Broken ON THE Back Row

Broken ON THE Back Row

A Journey through *Grace* and *Forgiveness*

SANDI PATTY

HOWARD
PUBLISHING CO.

This story is written solely because God is the God of second chances.

It is dedicated to the Lord of my life,

the sustainer of my soul,

the comforter of my pain,

and the healer of my wounds:

Jesus, the Christ.

It is now, has always been, and forever will be only about Him.

What a God . . . what a journey . . . what a SAVIOR!

Our purpose at Howard Publishing is to:
Increase faith in the hearts of growing Christians
Inspire holiness in the lives of believers
Instill hope in the hearts of struggling people everywhere
Because He's coming again!

Broken on the Back Row © 2005 by Sandi Patty
All rights reserved. Printed in the United States of America
Published by Howard Publishing Co., Inc.
3117 North 7th Street, West Monroe, Louisiana 71291-2227

ISBN 1-58229-426-7

Scripture not otherwise marked is from the HOLY BIBLE, NEW INTERNATIONAL VERSION ®. Copyright © 1973, 1978, 1984 by International Bible Society. Used by permission of Zondervan Publishing House. All rights reserved. Scriptures marked NASB are taken from the NEW AMERICAN STANDARD BIBLE®, copyright © 1960, 1962, 1963, 1968, 1971, 1972, 1973, 1975, 1977, 1995 by The Lockman Foundation. Used by permission.

For more information about Sandi Patty, go to www.sandipatty.com
For bookings, contact:
William Morris Agency
1600 Division Street, Suite 300
Nashville, TN 37203
615-963-3000

Management information:
Mike Atkins Entertainment
615-345-4554

CONTENTS

ACKNOWLEDGMENTS

I wish to thank my family:

My parents, RON AND CAROLYN PATTY, who have modeled for
me the unconditional love of Christ

My brothers, MIKE AND CRAIG, who tolerated and helped temper
their bossy big sister

My best friend, partner in life, and husband, DON. Thank you for
your love and for showing me how beautiful I am in your eyes

Our children, ANNA, JON, JEN, ERIN, DONNIE, ALY, MOLLIE, AND
SAM for your patience, wisdom, and laughter that fill our home
and my heart with joy.

I thank my pastor, JIM LYON, AND MY CHURCH FAMILY at the
North Anderson Church of God for giving me sanctuary in my
storm. For nurturing our family, even today. For giving me a place
to cry, laugh, learn, and grow—a place to continue the journey of
becoming all God wants me to be.

ACKNOWLEDGMENTS

A very big thank-you to my friend and manager, MIKE ATKINS. You make Herb proud!

Thank you, KIMMIE, for always dotting the i's and crossing the t's.

And to my friend SUE ANN JONES for helping me put words to my heart. Thank you hardly covers it, but it will have to do: thank you!

FOREWORD
BY MAX LUCADO

Many remember their first encounter with the voice of Sandi Patty. I know I can. It flows like a whitewater river: clean, fresh, soothing. You don't forget Sandi's voice.

But her voice is nothing compared to her heart.

It's had its tough times, this heart of Sandi. Guilt, hurt, anger, fear—her heart has felt it all. Yet, through it all, she has continued to sing. If your heart is finding it hard to do the same, my friend Sandi can help. She gently tutors the brokenhearted on the pages of this book. Honestly, transparently, she shares her life experience and her path to confession and restitution.

She reminds us that repentance can be a tough process. Her story is a classic tale of pain surmounted by God's grace and forgiveness, often demonstrated by the Christlike people God placed in her life.

I love Sandi as a sister in Christ. She's weathered her share of struggles—some deserved, some not. Through it all she is emerging with deeper faith in God and tender compassion for all. Sandi is a minister. Through song and spirit, she helps us see Christ and the grace that is available, even to the brokenhearted on the back row.

A NOTE TO YOU
BEFORE YOU BEGIN

Thank you for your interest in my book. Before you begin, I want to put a few facts on the table so you won't feel shocked or misled halfway through.

If you know me only as Sandi Patty, Christian entertainer—or recording artist, as we call ourselves in the industry—I want you to know there have been some chapters in my life that will probably disappoint and possibly even anger you. Before you judge me by my music as someone to be admired, let me warn you that I've already let you down.

I've made some poor choices and foolish mistakes in my life.

Big-time mistakes.

I committed adultery—and told lies to cover it up. I went through a divorce, and now I'm nearly ten years into a very happy second marriage.

This book is the story of my journey from devastating sin through healing forgiveness and into God's incredible grace. It's the story of the difficult steps I had to take to regain wholeness and restoration to the body of Christ. And finally, it's the glorious story of how the truth has set me free.

If you're looking for bitter accusations and excuses about why my first marriage failed, you won't find them here. In the breakup of any marriage, there are—or at least there should be—issues that are private and are not put on display for public consideration. Don't expect to find lurid details of the affair I was involved in either. It happened. I've acknowledged it, apologized one-on-one to the individuals I harmed by my actions, and been forgiven by God and restored to my church.

I share my story now, not to refresh your memory of the scandal I caused more than a decade ago, but so you might see anew the mercy and power and goodness of our God, the God of second chances. I want you to know that what He did for me, He can also do for you.

If this isn't the book you were expecting, now's the time to return it and ask for your money back. I apologize for disappointing you and for any hurt I might have caused you.

On the other hand, if you've also made mistakes in your life and you long for restoration and wholeness, I hope you'll come along and share my journey. It follows a well-traveled spiritual pathway that leads from sin and deceitfulness right up to Calvary, where our Savior died so we could know forgiveness, grace, and unconditional love.

That's where you'll find me today, gathered with all the others who've been forgiven and redeemed, gratefully clinging forever to the foot of that old rugged cross.

—Sandi Patty

Prologue

THE BACK ROW OF
THE BALCONY

In the backseat the younger three kids—toddler Erin in her safety seat and the kindergartner twins, Jonathan and Jennifer, sitting beside her—were quiet, for once. They didn't understand why yet another change had to happen in their lives, but they trusted me to keep them safe and make things OK. Beside me in the front seat, my oldest child, Anna, a second-grader, kept up a cheerful running commentary, speculating on which friends she might see that morning.

I gripped the steering wheel with one hand and chewed a fingernail on the other, a little nervous about what I was doing but knowing it was necessary. In that season of my life, I felt very far away from God. It was not a comfortable place to be, but it was nobody's fault but my own. Wrong and sinful choices do that; they move you further away from God.

To look at me that day, you probably wouldn't have known there was a problem. If you had known me then, you probably would have thought I was a woman with a successful music career, honored with more awards than any other contemporary Christian vocalist, the eleven-time recipient of the Dove Award for Female Vocalist of the Year. You probably would have thought I had everything going for me.

You probably wouldn't have known that my life was crashing in on all sides.

Separated from my husband, with divorce proceedings pending, I was learning how to be a single mom of four young children. I was worried that the divorce would damage my career—and even more worried that the press would uncover the terrible secret I was hiding. I was terrified that my kids would be hurt by all the poor choices I had made.

Our family had been going to the same church for years. It was a good church. But I needed to find a new place for myself where I could grow and learn. I had heard some good things about the new pastor at North Anderson Church of God, and that Sunday morning I had decided to take the kids and go.

I talked to them about it beforehand, about how they would go to Sunday school and I would go to "big church." They had a few friends at the new church, so that would make things easier. As I drove there that morning, I thought that even if I didn't enjoy the service, at least I would have a quiet hour to myself. Those of you with young children know what I'm talking about.

Walking across the parking lot, moving with the crowds through the door and into the lobby, I hoped no one would recognize me. I felt like I had a big scarlet letter across my chest—an

A for adulterer, and maybe an *L* too, for liar. I avoided any eye contact, feeling sure that everybody there knew about the sin in my life.

I put the kids in Sunday school and happened to pass by the door leading to the balcony. Without really thinking about it, I started up the stairs. There weren't any empty seats down in front, so I kept climbing. Finally I found a seat in the back row of the balcony, right under the huge stained-glass window, and that's where I sat.

As soon as I settled onto the pew, I became very emotional. The choir started singing, and I cried. A baby was dedicated, and I cried. A teenager was baptized, and I cried. They took up the offering, and I cried. It was just a very emotional morning for me. I knew I had an hour or so to let the tears flow; then I would have to pull myself together in time to pick up the kids and go home.

As the service ended, the pastor came down from the pulpit and took a few steps down one of the aisles of the large, airy sanctuary.

"If you're visiting with us today, we're so glad you're here," he said, his pleasant voice ringing out warmly. All of a sudden a spike of dread caused me to tense. I dug into my purse for another tissue. *Oh, please don't make the visitors stand up. Don't have someone hand me a rose. I can't do that. Not today,* I thought.

But the pastor continued, "We're so happy to have you here," he said again. Then he added, "There are people all around you who would like to know your name, if you would like to tell them. We want you to know that the God we serve lives within these walls—and outside these walls too."

He took a few more steps down the aisle and looked all around the crowded sanctuary. "But maybe you've been visiting with us here this morning, and you're not ready to tell anyone your name. Maybe all you want to do is sit on the back row of the balcony and cry. That's OK," he said. "We want you to know that the God we serve knows how to find you there. He hasn't forgotten about you. We serve the God of second chances, the God of new beginnings. We serve the God who sets His children free."

Later that insightful pastor, Jim Lyon, would tell me he hadn't noticed me sitting in the balcony, crying my eyes out, during the service. He didn't know I was there. But God knew. And He had placed those words on Pastor Lyon's heart that morning so that when I heard them, I would know He had already found me there, broken on the back row of the balcony.

That day began a journey for me. A journey back toward Him.

The melody that He gave to me
Within my heart is ringing.
—C. Austin Miles
"In the Garden"

Chapter One

MUSIC IN MY GENES

I grew up in church, and my childhood was infused with gospel music. My dad was a minister of music throughout all my growing-up years, and my mom was (and still is) a wonderful pianist. Every Sunday morning, Sunday night, and Wednesday evening, my two younger brothers and I had to sit on the "front row, piano side," as my fellow preacher's-kid friend Chonda Pierce likes to say.

Mom would make sure the piano was placed so she could see my dad, who was leading the singing, and so she could also signal to us kids with her left hand. Mom had a very expressive range of hand motions; she probably could have landed planes with her left hand! She would be playing along, and my brothers and I would start messing around, and she would meander down to the lower registers of the keyboard during whatever hymn she was playing and *snap!* her fingers under our noses. Then she would go right back to playing the rest of the song as if nothing had happened. It was always amazing to us how she could do so many things at once. And we were absolutely in awe of her 360-degree vision. She had eyes not only on the back of her head but also on the sides and the top. We rarely got away with anything.

My parents loved God and made music their gift to Him. They both grew up in Oklahoma but met in college in Indiana. My dad, Ron Patty, came from a musical and athletic family. Dad excelled in sports and in playing the trumpet. He was offered a trumpet scholarship to Tulsa University and a football scholarship to Oklahoma University but turned them down to attend Anderson University (it was Anderson College until more recently, but for simplicity's sake I'll call it AU throughout this book); it's a wonderful Church of God school in Anderson, Indiana.

AU awarded Dad football and baseball scholarships plus a job as custodian at the gymnasium, so almost all his expenses were paid. While he was in school, the Dodgers, then based in Brooklyn, New York, recruited him for the pros, but he turned them down. In addition to those two sports, he was exceptionally talented as a fast-pitch softball pitcher and played on several teams that won world championships. While he was in school he also performed with a gospel music quartet, the Christian Brothers. And guess who was the quartet's pianist!

My mom, Carolyn Tunnel Patty, came from an equally talented and hard-working family. Her dad was a pastor who had brought his wife and three children to Indiana so he could attend AU during the Great Depression. It must have been a lofty goal at that time to want a college degree, but education has always been important to my family. My grandparents settled in Shelbyville, a little town outside of Anderson, where Mom's father pastored a little church for $10 a week—$520 a year. Three days a week, he drove into town to attend classes at AU. My mom was six years old at the time, and she remembers that occasionally he would bring her with him to the university. She loved all the sights and sounds of being on a bustling college campus.

To help make ends meet, Mom's mother took in mending. Times were hard for everyone back then. Men who couldn't afford to buy new clothes paid my grandmother to take the frayed collars off their shirts and turn them around so the edges were smooth again. She also attended a few classes at the college.

It was during this time that a struggling piano teacher walked from house to house in Shelbyville, knocking on doors and asking, "Do you have a child you would like to have piano lessons?"

The teacher offered a buy-one-get-one-free deal. For fifty cents a week, a child could have two lessons. As poor as my grandparents were, they found the money for music. In doing so, they gave my mother a wonderful lifetime gift. She started those lessons at age six, with her daddy sitting beside her each day to practice, and she kept taking lessons right through college, when she was a piano major at Anderson University. With her natural talent and extensive training, she could have become a concert pianist. Instead, she opted for a career as a stay-at-home wife and mother who sometimes traveled with my dad when he was touring with various groups to perform at churches, auditoriums, camp meetings, and all sorts of other gatherings.

As poor as my grandparents were, they found the money for music.

How blessed I've been by this legacy of love and music!

Mom met my dad when they were both students at AU. They were married on June 5, 1953, at a church near campus. Dad was playing fast-pitch softball that summer, and his team just happened to have a game that night. Being a committed athlete (and with the support of my mother), Dad wore his uniform under his wedding tuxedo! As soon as he could slip away from the wedding reception, he took off his wedding clothes, pulled on his cleats and cap, and rushed to the ballpark. That night he pitched a perfect game, which means that no one on the other team even reached first base. (Dad says he was in a bit of a hurry that night; otherwise he might have let the opponents have at least one hit.)

All that explains why, when Mom and Dad renewed their vows at a chapel on the AU campus fifty years later, the recessional wasn't the usual "Wedding March." Instead the organist played, "Take Me Out to the Ball Game"!

A Growing Love of Family—and Music

Before they could finish college, Dad was offered a job as minister of music at a church back home in Oklahoma, so off they went to Oklahoma City. In addition to his new job there, Dad continued to tour occasionally with music groups, including the extraordinarily popular choral group called the Pennsylvanians, which was directed by the late Fred Waring, who earned the Congressional Gold Medal and was known as "the Man Who Taught America to Sing."

Mom sometimes accompanied Dad when she was needed to play the piano for a touring group, but it wasn't long before

I came along to complicate her travel plans. At one point Dad toured with the group for a three-month stretch, leaving Mom at home to take care of me. It was much too long for him to be away from us, and they both agreed that Dad wouldn't accept such a long-term touring invitation again.

He accepted *some* invitations, however. When Fred Waring and the Pennsylvanians were invited to perform at the White House for President Dwight Eisenhower and a special guest—Queen Elizabeth—Dad was there lending his voice to that heavenly sound. Mom stayed behind in Oklahoma because she had a toddler to tend to (me) and because she was pregnant with my brother Mike.

Stepping into the Spotlight

I made my musical debut in Oklahoma City at the age of two and a half, when my dad lifted me onto a table he had dragged next to the podium. I belted out a stirring rendition of "Jesus Loves Me." The voice was there, according to my parents, but my stage presence wasn't quite developed yet. Somewhere in the middle of the song, my Patty grandparents arrived, having driven in from Sapulpa, Oklahoma, especially to hear my first solo. My face lit up when I saw them, and I stopped singing and called out, "Hi, Grandma!" Then I took a breath and finished the song. By all accounts (at least the way my parents tell it), I brought down the house.

To nurture my interest in music, Mom bought me a little record player when I was just three or four. "I wanted you to have something you could use to play music yourself," she told me later.

"So many parents have fancy stereos or other audio equipment that their children aren't allowed to touch. I wanted you to be able to play records and enjoy the music on your own, whenever and however you wanted to hear it. So I found that little metal record player and some records—probably nursery rhymes or other children's songs—that you could operate yourself, and you would spend hours playing and singing along to that music."

Mom also remembered that one of my full-time jobs was keeping the record player away from my little brother Mike.

To be honest, I don't remember that fledgling beginning of my musical career. My earliest memory is of my dad pulling me on a little sled through the snow one Oklahoma winter day. It's a unique memory, because that would be the last time I would see snow until I moved to Indiana several years later to attend college. From Oklahoma, my parents moved to Phoenix, and we said good-bye to cold, snowy weather for a long time.

When I was five and a half, Mom did for me what her parents had done for her. She started me on piano lessons.

In Phoenix my dad was again working as the minister of music at a large church. Its choir, which Dad directed, even had a Sunday afternoon television program called *Songs over the Desert*. When I was five or six years old, Dad invited me to do a solo for that program. He brought in my little single-size bed from home to create a set. I wore my cutest pajamas and knelt beside the bed, hands pressed together under my chin, while I sang "A Child's Prayer" in front of the cameras.

I wasn't a bit nervous. Singing was such a part of my life by then that it was almost as natural as speaking. Music was always playing—or being sung—in the Patty household. And wherever we went in the car, we sang. Dad tells a story about riding in the car and singing with Mom, Mike, and me when I was very young and being puzzled when I suddenly went off key.

What in the world? Dad mused. *Has she suddenly gone tone deaf?*

But then I finally found the notes I was instinctively looking for, and Dad understood what I was struggling to do. "She was making up a part," he likes to say. "As young as she was, she was creating a harmony."

I tell you these things not to brag but to show you that yes, I've had a lot of voice training over the years, but it all started with the God-given gifts of good genes and devoted parents. I did nothing to deserve such gifts; God simply gave them to me. Without those blessings, my life would have followed a completely different path.

Occasionally Dad would spend a week or two traveling with one of his regular touring groups. Mom was usually home, although a few times she arranged for us to stay with friends from church for a few days when Dad and his fellow vocalists needed her to come along as the pianist.

Partners in Piano

When I was five and a half, Mom did for me what her parents had done for her. She started me on piano lessons.

"I started your mother on the piano because *I* wanted to," she tells my children now. "I taught her myself until she turned six. Then I took her to the best piano teacher I could find in Phoenix."

And every day, just as her dad had done with her, Mom sat with me as I practiced. "It was just like a parent sits with children to make sure they get their homework right," she explains. "I would sit beside Sandi and help her when she needed it. I made her practice, just as my parents made me practice. I had no choice, and neither did she. But it was a pleasant thing. I loved it, and I think she enjoyed it too, for the most part. She never did fight me about practicing. We practiced together; then, when I saw that she had her lesson down pat, I would go into the kitchen and start fixing supper, but my ear was always tuned in to her. I wanted to help her all that I could."

If I didn't say it then, I certainly will say it now: thanks, Mom!

A Family on Tour

A few years later, after the arrival of my second brother, Craig, we moved again, this time to beautiful San Diego. Dad was hired as both senior pastor and minister of music at a church there, and we happily settled into life in Southern California.

Mom continued to encourage my interest in piano, and amazingly, she bought a grand piano for my brothers and me to share with her while we were still at home. For years we'd had a Cable Nelson spinet piano that had served our family well. But remember: Mom had the skill of a concert pianist, and although she never put any expectations on us, I guess she could see that her children had inherited some of her and dad's musical talent. So when I was in ninth grade, she traded in the Cable Nelson for a good-quality, used Steinway. It took her three years of teaching piano lessons at two or three dollars a lesson to pay off the balance at a hundred dollars a month, but to this day she insists it was worth every hard-earned dollar to bring that fabulous piano into our home. And as far as I know, no one argues with her about it!

Music filled my high-school days. I was active in choir and madrigals at Crawford High School in San Diego, and I played the part of Maria in the drama department's production of *West Side Story*. What a thrill that was! Besides all the musical events, I was on the school's volleyball team and was a cheerleader for the football and basketball teams. Meanwhile my brothers were busy learning a variety of musical instruments in band. (Mom had made sure they had some piano lessons as well.)

At some point—no one can remember exactly when—we tried blending all our talents and doing a couple of songs together as a family. As Mom says now, "It wasn't too bad." I can just imagine the looks that were exchanged over our heads by Mom and Dad as they heard us "perform" for the first time. Accustomed to performing with musical groups, they decided to take us on the road. The next thing my brothers and I knew, we were spending a couple of weeks each summer traveling around America entertaining church groups with our parents as the Ron Patty Family. We would go all over California, through the Southwest, and then back east to Indiana, Pennsylvania, Ohio, and New York before singing our way home by a different route.

"We had been traveling and working in churches for so long, we had lots of contacts," my mom explains. "So before we started out each summer, we would call these churches and ask if they would like to have a concert. Almost all of them said yes, so we would book the dates and hit the road."

We left after church on Sunday and spent two weeks on the

road during Dad's vacation time. That way he only had to be away from the church he pastored for one Sunday. The five of us traveled in a big, rented RV that also towed a large trailer containing all our equipment. We took *everything* we needed for the concert: not just lights and sound equipment but also a piano, an organ, and a drum set, as well as timpani (the big kettle drums my brother Craig played). We even took our own stage! So everywhere we performed, we would wheel in all the instruments, along with plywood and cinderblocks for building the platform. Then Mom would snap a purple stage skirt onto the plywood to cover up the blocks. Purple was our theme color. My mom and I wore purple dresses; I wore white vinyl go-go boots, while Mom opted for dressy pumps. My brothers wore black pants and purple shirts with black sweater vests, and my dad wore a purple cardigan. Oh, we looked *fine*!

My dad had learned a lot about pacing and programming from his years of performing with Fred Waring and the Pennsylvanians and other gospel music groups. He and Mom organized our concerts by arranging songs around themes; then they varied the tempo of the musical selections and featured different family members on the various songs. I played the organ, Mom played the piano, Mike played the drums, Craig played the timpani, Dad was the lead vocalist, and we all joined in on different singing parts.

Dad set up the program so that some songs were introduced with a brief story or sidebar, but other times one song flowed right into the next. My parents really knew how to put on a show. No wonder churches invited us back year after year! All they had to do was open their doors and welcome us in, and we took it from there, singing God's praises in churches coast to coast. We even performed in Alaska and Hawaii—without the RV and trailer, of course. We also did a lot of individual concerts on weekends, especially close to home on Sunday nights so that Dad could be at our church on Sunday mornings.

When we were traveling in the RV, we occasionally stayed in motels. Every Monday Mom would head off to a Laundromat to wash our clothes. She likes to tell the story that we traveled to Florida and made a stopover at Walt Disney World shortly after the amusement park opened. All of America was dying to go to Orlando and visit that amazing place. But I, being a teenager, opted to stay in the motel and sleep. Now Mom teases me whenever I'm invited to perform at one of the Disney parks, reminding me that I didn't know what I was missing all those years ago.

My mom and I wore purple dresses; I wore white vinyl go-go boots, while Mom opted for dressy pumps.

But you know how teenagers are. I needed my sleep! And sometimes it was impossible to get any when we were all crowded into the RV or a single motel room. We paid our way on these summer tours by taking up a goodwill offering and also by selling albums and eight-track tapes of our music. We had made the recordings at a private studio, and while we bought the albums (and we're talking vinyl records here, folks) from the studio, my brother made all our eight-track tapes, copying them himself on a special quick-recording machine. We all had jobs, and that was his. Whenever we would spend a night in a motel room, Craig would plug in the eight-track machine and start making tapes. The problem was that the machine made a LOUD click each time the tape moved from one track to the next, and I found that to be the most irritating sound in the world. While I was trying to get my beauty rest, Craig would be over there at the desk clicking and clacking away. I probably made almost as much noise with all my sighs and groans of complaint as the machine did with its clicks and clacks.

The prices for our tapes and albums ranged from three to five dollars each. Mom's job at each stop was to head into town before the concert and get the money we would need to make change at the product table. After each performance we all worked at the table to sell our merchandise and greet the audience members. Then it was time to pack up the trailer, climb into the RV, and head to the next town.

Laying the Groundwork

All of us look back on those days with great fondness, laughing about mishaps and rolling our eyes as we "kids" remember each other's goofy antics. Oh, it wasn't always fun, of course. The RV would occasionally break down. And let's be honest: having five people live in one RV for two weeks tends to result in a little crankiness now and then, especially when three of the five people are adolescents! But there was plenty of laughter and lots of love packed into that motor home too.

It was a wonderful time of togetherness and sharing. And although I could never have imagined it back then, it was an experience I would repeat again and again on my own, in various forms, later in my life. Those summers with my family—living in the rented RV, pulling the equipment trailer, performing for audiences around the country—laid a foundation I would build on for decades to come. Even today I arrange my concerts along the guidelines Dad used when he was putting together the program for our family concerts.

While we were traveling as a family, my brother Craig taught me to spy on the audience, and it's something I still do to this day. When Craig was just eight or nine years old, he used to hide somewhere out of sight and listen to the sounds in the auditorium so he could predict what the audience would be like that night. "If there's a general hum, with lots of talking, but you can't pick out individual voices, you know there are lots of people there. If you can hear individual voices and there's no hum, then the audience is smaller," Craig would say.

I've used his idea all these years since then. Before every concert I'll find a spot for my spying activities. I like to see without being seen, but if that's not possible, I'll just find a spot where I can listen. If the audience is subdued, I know it will be a quieter evening. But if there's lot of laughter and the place is humming, I know it's going to be a fun show. Sometimes I'll even change the musical lineup based on what I hear from the audience during these preshow episodes. I'll tell my piano player and sound man something like, "OK, we need to start with this instead of that, and in the second half, let's skip this one and do that one instead."

I picked up a lot of tips and guidelines from Dad that I use frequently in my concerts today. But I didn't know back then that I was learning anything that would be useful in my future. During those long summer road trips, whenever I curled up to daydream on a bunk as Dad drove the RV with Mom sitting beside him as navigator, I pictured myself as a future teacher sharing the joys and marvels of music with students in some local high school or college.

I could never have imagined what lay in wait for me just a few years down the road.

Many things about tomorrow
I don't seem to understand;
But I know who holds tomorrow,
And I know who holds my hand.
—Ira F. Stanphill
"I Know Who Holds Tomorrow"

Chapter Two

AN ARTIST BY ACCIDENT

Warmed by the many hugs and kisses of my parents and brothers as I said good-bye, I took the red-eye flight from San Diego and arrived in Indianapolis at dawn one morning in August 1974. Still a teenager and a bit reluctant to leave my close-knit family, I had come to Indiana alone to enroll in Anderson University. I'd brought along a couple of big suitcases and a heart full of hope that I could complete what seemed like a giant step into the future.

The AU shuttle was scheduled to pick me up at the airport, but a funny thing happened. As I was waiting for my luggage, I ran into another AU student I had met the previous summer when my family was traveling. We had done a concert at his church, and he had told me then that he would be a senior at AU in the fall. He was at the airport picking up some of his friends who would also be students. When he asked if I had a ride to school, I told him I was scheduled to take the shuttle. "Forget that!" he said. "Why don't you just go with us?" And with that I met my first friends at AU. They brought me to Anderson, about an hour's drive away, and delivered me to my dorm. Interestingly, one of those new friends was Steve Brallier, who later became one of my agents at William Morris.

Although the town is two thousand miles from San Diego, I had been there several times before. The headquarters for the Church of God, my family's church for several generations, is based in Anderson, and AU is a Church of God school. The denomination's annual Camp Meeting is held on the college campus, and my family had attended several times.

Interestingly, freshman boys had no curfew. I guess they figured if the girls were in, the guys would be in too.

Frankly, I had never found the campus very appealing during those gatherings because the place was packed with so many people it was hard to get anywhere or do anything without encountering huge crowds. I had about decided to attend Warner Pacific College, another Church of God school in Portland, Oregon, when I happened to visit AU at a time when the Camp Meeting was not in session. I couldn't believe how fabulous it was! The rolling lawns, beautiful trees, friendly students, devoted faculty, and appealing course offerings—I fell in love with the place and have loved it ever since.

Because it was a church school, there were a few restrictions, of course. For starters, freshman girls had to be in their dorms by ten o'clock on weeknights and by midnight on weekends. Interestingly, freshman boys had no curfew. I guess they figured if the girls were in, the guys would be in too.

There were no school-sponsored dances, and of course no alcohol was allowed on campus. But none of those prohibitions bothered me. I was just delighted to be on the same campus where my parents and grandparents had worked and played and studied. I loved visiting the athletic fields where my dad had played in front of cheering crowds. And visiting the gym, where he had been employed as a custodian, brought a loving appreciation for how hard he had worked.

I planned to follow in my mother's footsteps and study piano; in fact my primary piano teacher had been Mom's teacher at the college too. I enjoyed the piano, but my overall goal was to acquire my teaching credentials so I could teach in public schools.

I loved my newfound independence, and I was thrilled to see the change of the seasons slowly paint the beautiful campus with the brilliant spectrum of autumn, something we didn't see in Southern California. There is nothing like walking through a gentle shower of golden maple leaves as they flutter to the ground in a September breeze. I was completely enthralled with Indiana.

Then came the first snow. It's a phenomenon I enjoy to this day, the first snowfall of the season. When those big, fluffy flakes swirl through the neighborhood, blanketing everything with a quiet muffler of cottony white, I still love to cuddle up beside a window and watch as the world is magically transformed. (Of course, my attitude has changed completely by the time that last, freakishly late winter storm comes barreling through in April.) To a California girl accustomed to constant sunshine and warm, balmy ocean breezes, that first beautiful snow in 1974 was a mystical, magical event, frozen forever in my mind as a beautiful memory.

Then reality set in. My dormitory was on one side of campus, and the piano practice rooms were on the other. After a few weeks of battling bitter winds, icy sidewalks, and/or mounds of slush to get to a piano every day, I had a brilliant idea: I would change my academic emphasis to voice! Then all I would need was a pitch pipe, and I could practice in my dorm room.

Now, to you this might seem like the ultimate in wimpiness. But I like to think it was God's hand adjusting my career path.

A Change of Plans

As much as I loved AU, I missed my family. And I felt as though I had let down my parents and brothers just as our family was at its peak in traveling together and performing gospel music concerts. Before I left home, Dad had been inviting me, with growing frequency, to do more solos during the concerts or to sing duets with him in performances or at the church where he continued to serve as pastor and minister of music. I remember, in particular, how as a child I had listened in awe as he and one of the choir members sang a special duet, "It Took a Miracle." Hearing the beautiful lyrics and the soaring melody, I had dreamed of singing that duet with Dad. In the last year before I left home, we had started doing the song together in concerts. It was hard to think I wouldn't enjoy that special sharing for a long time to come.

I struggled with indecision. But then, at the end of the first semester, torn by conflicting loyalties to my family and my love of AU, I returned home and enrolled in San Diego State. I lived at home and quickly became involved in the music and drama departments and was tapped for one of the solo roles in the Christmas performance of Handel's *Messiah*. Later I won the role of the comic-relief character in *How to Succeed in Business without Really Trying*. During the summers I did concerts with my family, and on weekends I performed in a little band at wedding receptions and parties with my brother Mike and some friends. I also worked part time for a junior-high music teacher, an experience that solidified my desire to become a teacher myself.

It felt good to be back with my family, but I missed the independence I'd enjoyed briefly at Anderson University; in San Diego State's huge student population, I felt lost compared with the closeness I'd enjoyed back at AU. Plus, because I was living at home, I didn't have much of a social life. Embarrassed by indecisiveness but determined to make a decision and stick with it, in 1977 I transferred back to Anderson, determined to finish up my degree at AU. It was the right decision. I've been here ever since.

Influenced by Others

People who would influence my life in a big way started crossing my path once I was back in Anderson. For instance, there was Greta Dominique, an AU faculty member who seemed to work magic with all of her aspiring vocalist students. Gradually, with Greta's coaching, my voice took on a whole new range, endurance, and quality.

My mom is now a close friend of Greta's, and they laugh about what happened to me under her direction. Mom says Greta insists she doesn't know exactly what she did to help me "open up my throat," but whatever it was, we're all happy she did it! Sometimes after she had directed me through yet another vocal exercise, we would just look at each other, both a little stunned by what we had heard, as though it were coming from a third person in the practice room. (And, of course, it was. I've never said my voice was anything except a gift from my gracious and generous God. But who knew He was a soprano?)

In addition to Greta, I began rubbing shoulders with other people who enjoyed singing, including, of course, other students. I tried out for an AU touring group called New Nature and was delighted to be accepted. There were six of us singers—three guys and three girls—and another guy who ran sound for us. The sound guy, John Helvering, was the one who caught my eye and held my attention. A short while later, I would marry him.

But I had plenty of other things to keep me busy besides romance. New Nature traveled to performances during the school year and the summer; we even made a record that we sold at our concerts. I also had several part-time jobs. I became the church pianist for the East Side Church of God, playing for their church services and accompanying their choir and children's choir. And I began giving piano lessons to area youngsters as a way to earn a little extra money. Two of my students were the kids of a couple my parents had met through their music tours. Perhaps you know them too: Bill and Gloria Gaither.

When I wasn't studying or practicing or working, I was hanging out at another little studio, Burlap Sound, near the AU campus.

The Gaithers, a little younger than my parents, had also attended AU, and they lived in a nearby town. My dad likes to tell how Bill used to pitch his songs to the group my dad was singing with in college, the Christian Brothers Quartet. I guess the guys didn't use many of Bill's songs, but they enjoyed getting acquainted with him anyway. By the time I arrived on campus nearly twenty years later, the Gaithers were becoming stars in the world of Christian music. But they took the time to be very involved with and supportive of their alma mater, and I enjoyed getting acquainted with them. Before long they were sending their kids to me for piano lessons.

As we got to know each other a little better, they asked me to do some studio work for them, singing backup for many of the clients who had chosen to record their projects at the Gaithers' studio. I worked in Indianapolis studios as well, singing commercial jingles for products such as Juicy Fruit gum and Steak n Shake restaurants. And I helped with background vocals for various recording artists and groups. I loved the work—really loved it. When I wasn't studying or practicing or working, I was hanging out at another little studio, Burlap Sound, near the AU campus. I was new to the business, and the engineer there was new as well, so we learned about the recording process together as we helped clients complete their projects.

It was all fun. But it was nothing more than that—an enjoyable way to earn a little extra spending money. I still thought of myself as a teacher-to-be. Being around music throughout my life, I had seen too many people surviving hand-to-mouth because all they could focus on was becoming an artist in the music industry. I didn't want that kind of unstable existence. I longed for the kind of rock-solid, secure family environment my mom and dad had created for my brothers and me. I wanted the same priorities they had always demonstrated: faith, family, friends, and work. There was no way I would ever become one of those people whose life was completely dominated by career aspirations. Huh-uh. Not me.

"Take Five Minutes"

This it's-only-a-hobby attitude continued as my parents invited me to perform with them whenever one of their tours happened to come within five hundred miles or so of Anderson. Now that my brothers were able to fend for themselves, Mom and Dad traveled more frequently with these different gospel music tours, and they also arranged and directed the music for the Bill Glass Crusades.

Bill Glass, a college football all-American and former all-pro player with the Cleveland Browns, is an evangelist who has a special heart for prison ministries. His organization, now called Champions for Life, sponsors huge citywide crusades, held in arenas and football stadiums, that bring together Christians from many denominations to celebrate the love of Christ and to inspire a positive impact on the community. While I was in college, Mom and Dad organized the choirs, managed the musical programming, and helped perform the special music for these crusades. And whenever they were within range of me—anywhere in Ohio, Illinois, Indiana, or Michigan—I met them to join the musical portion of the program.

Dad loves to tell the story of the first time I came out with them on the crusade, and he asked me to "take five minutes" and sing a solo. The next time I met up with the crusade, he asked me to take ten minutes. Before long I had a fifteen-minute segment in the musical lineup. We laugh about it now because whenever Mom and Dad can join me at a concert within easy traveling distance of Anderson, where we all live today, I say, "Dad, why don't you take five minutes and do something with me in the concert?"

I even recorded an album of my own in the Burlap Sound Studio so I would have something to sell at the crusade product tables. It was called *For My Friends,* and I sold it not only at the crusades but also at the increasing number of events where I was invited to sing around Anderson. I had done privately produced records with my family for our summer tours, and I had recorded the album with the New Nature group. Still, it seemed a little ostentatious to have a record all my own. It's hard to explain how you can be proud of something and embarrassed by it at the same time. I guess I was imagining that someday my future music students would find an old, dusty copy of the record hidden in some classroom and giggle, thinking their teacher had gone through a phase as a wannabe music star. Still, the records seemed to sell well wherever I performed, so while singing still seemed more of a hobby than anything else, it was becoming a profitable hobby.

Caught Up in the Whirlwind

Meanwhile I had fallen in love, and the music I wanted to hear most of all was wedding bells. Suddenly I felt a great urgency to be finished with college so I could move on to the next stage of my life as a wife and life partner to my husband-to-be. Because I had transferred back and forth to San Diego State, I had a lot of college credits, but not all of them had been accepted toward my AU degree. (I tell people I crammed four years of college into five.) Going into my senior year in 1978, I lacked a couple of classes for the degree in music education, plus I still had to do my student teaching and complete some other requirements.

I didn't want to leave school without a degree. I had seen how that situation had hung over my parents' heads all their lives after they dropped out of college so Dad could accept the job as music minister in Oklahoma City. They had invested a lot in me, and I had worked hard. I wanted that diploma! But it was starting to look like I would need an extra semester to get everything wrapped up, and I didn't want to do that.

I was too young to see the potential for problems, too naive to be aware of the emotional baggage I was bringing into the marriage.

I went to my adviser and laid out the problem. "What can I do to get a degree by next spring?" I asked.

"Well, Sandi, looking at your transcript, it seems that most of your credits are in conducting," she said. "Would you want to go for a degree in that?"

"Conducting it is!" I replied, disappointed to give up my dream of becoming a teacher but relieved to find a way out of the dilemma.

With that plan in place, I set about making other plans—including arrangements for a November 1978 wedding. While it was true that my fiancé and I hadn't dated all that long, we felt sure that ours was the love of a lifetime. Unwilling to consider that it might be wise to wait, at least until I graduated, I rushed into marriage, completely confident that soon I would be enjoying the same loving, nurturing, devoted relationship I had seen my parents share throughout my life. What an exciting time that was, a season of eager anticipation for the certain joy that lay ahead.

I was too young to see the potential for problems, too naive to be aware of the emotional baggage I was bringing into the marriage, too much in love to see anything but the young man who would be waiting for me at the other end of the aisle as the wedding began.

But before that event took place, a different turning point popped up in front of me. In early November, one week before my wedding date, I met my parents in Martinsville, Indiana, to perform at another Bill Glass Crusade. At the end of the program, a man worked his way through the crowd and stuck out his hand. "I'm Phil Brower, Singspiration Music," he said, introducing himself to me. "Sandi, we would like to sign you to a record contract. Could you come to Grand Rapids next week?"

I couldn't believe what I was hearing. And I'm guessing Mr. Brower was also pretty surprised by my reply.

I said no.

In the morning light of God's creation
He reached from heaven to me.
Sweet miracle as He placed the flame of life inside
and carried an angel to me,
gave my soul a melody.
—Cindy Morgan, Jeff Lippencott, and Sandi Patty
"All This Time (Anna's Song)"

Chapter Three

THE HEAT OF THE SPOTLIGHT

By the middle of 1979, I thought I had everything a girl could want: a husband, a college degree—and a recording contract. While I'd turned down Phil Brower when he had approached me about a contract the previous November, I *had* met with Singspiration executives after the start of the new year. My husband and I had discussed the options, and knowing how brief a ride on the music bandwagon could be, we decided to take advantage of any opportunities for me to sing while they were offered. Enough doors seemed to be opening that it seemed this was the direction God was leading me.

Now I held in my hands the result of that contract, my first studio album produced by a major recording company: *Sandi's Song* on Milk and Honey Records, a Singspiration label. There was just one little problem: my last name had been misspelled as "Patti" on the promotional materials that went out in advance of the album. Someone somewhere had thought it would be cute, I guess, if both names ended in *i*. And because it seemed easier to let it go than to raise a fuss, I had allowed the spelling to be retained on the album itself. Although I felt a little sad about the mistake, I was swept up in all the excitement of this foray into the recording industry. And, to be honest, my name just didn't mean as much to me then as it does now. As a result, that misspelling—Sandi Patti—would appear on my next sixteen albums. Not until 1994, in the midst of the firestorm surrounding all the other mistakes I'd made, did I reclaim my rightful name and insist that it be spelled correctly, as Sandi Patty.

Now that *Sandi's Song* had been released, Singspiration was eager to introduce its new talent to the market. First the company took me to a print-music conference attended by five hundred ministers of music. Although I don't write a lot of music, I had written the title track, "Sandi's Song (My Life Is a Song)," and I performed it for that gathering.

It finally dawned on me that music wasn't just a fun hobby anymore.

I thought I saw someone in the audience yawning as I poured my heart into the song. The event drew little notice.

Next the record company took me to the Christian Booksellers Association convention in St. Louis. Phil Brower, the executive who had first proposed the contract, was the emcee of one of the evening concerts at the convention, and he introduced me as a new Singspiration talent making my debut.

Phil wanted to get the audiences's attention, so he suggested

I sing "Twinkle, Twinkle Little Star." But of course it wasn't just any old rendition of the nursery-rhyme song. With Don Wyrtzen accompanying me on the piano, I started out with a cute little jazzy rhythm and ended with a huge, operatic production. Having warmed up the crowd, I next sang a song off the album: "The Day He Wore My Crown." And when it was over, the fifteen hundred to two thousand convention attendees honored me with a standing ovation. I was blown away by their kindness.

Standing there on the stage, my head dropped in a stunned, awestruck bow as applause filled the room, I sent up silent words of gratitude and praise. *Thank You, God! I praise You, God, for Your gracious goodness to me.* And then I drew in a breath and blew it out slowly, feeling a change occur in my attitude toward the future. It finally dawned on me that music wasn't just a fun hobby anymore. *I guess we're really going to do this, aren't we, Lord?*

The Doves

Throughout the rest of 1979, I appeared occasionally with my parents, but I was also starting to do a few little church concerts on my own. Being a newlywed, I didn't relish the idea of being away from my husband, and I had already learned that there's a lot more to being a traveling musician than just getting up on the stage and singing. So it seemed logical for him to come along with me and be my manager. We would load up my performance tracks—the recorded accompaniment—and off we would go to whatever dates we had managed to book. The record label also set up some dates for us, and I was still doing some background vocals now and then at the Gaithers' studio, so I had occasional contact with Bill and Gloria.

One day Bill called and asked if I knew anyone with a soul-music kind of sound who would be willing to travel with the Gaither Trio as a backup singer.

"I need someone who can really sing some soul gospel music," he said.

I hesitated a moment, then asked, "Well, does this person have to be . . . black?" I didn't want to be disrespectful, but I couldn't think of any other way to say it.

"What are you thinking?" he asked.

I said, "I might be able to do that for you."

Someone had told Bill that I wasn't interested in traveling with the Gaithers. I couldn't believe it. Of *course* I was interested in traveling with one of the most popular vocal groups in Christian music!

So off we went, and the months flew by. In 1981 I made a second album, *Love Overflowing*, this time on the Benson label. On that album was the song "We Shall Behold Him." When he heard it, Bill Gaither asked me to "take five minutes" and perform the song as a solo at their concerts; before long he was inviting me to fill a little more time and sing a couple of other songs as well.

I was having a great time, traveling the country with my husband and the Gaithers, singing to others who loved the Lord just as I did. By the time I had collaborated with producer Greg Nelson to record a third album, *Lift Up the Lord*, I think I had finally accepted the idea that music had shifted from being my hobby to becoming my career. But I still didn't kid myself into thinking it was going to last forever.

When the Dove Award nominees were announced for 1982, I was absolutely dumbfounded to hear that my name was on the list—twice. I'd never been nominated for *anything*, and now I found myself being considered for the top award, Artist of the Year, as well as for Female Vocalist of the Year.

The Gospel Music Association (GMA) not only invited me to attend the awards evening as a nominee, it also asked me to sing "We Shall Behold Him" during the awards program itself. When the big night came, I found myself standing on stage, staring into the faces of the most famous and talented members of the Christian music community. It would have been glorious enough that evening just to be there and breathe the same air with all of them.

I sang the song, and soon after that, its creator, Dottie Rambo, was announced as the winner of the Dove Award for Songwriter of the Year. She laughed and told me after the program, "Thanks for taking my baby and dressing it up so pretty!"

The bestowing of awards continued, and unbelievably, when the awards for Female Vocalist of the Year and Artist of the Year were announced, it was *my* name that was called. I was overwhelmed with gratitude and emotion. To realize that these talented and dedicated artists were accepting me as their peer and recognizing me for my work was almost beyond my capacity to grasp. I floated onto the stage twice to accept the awards.

I have made several more trips onto that stage in the twenty-plus years since then, but no night could ever match the surprise and joy I felt that evening when those first Dove Awards were placed in my hands.

Anna, the Road Dog

I continued with the Gaithers awhile longer, loving our time together and gaining knowledge about the music business and touring that would serve me well in the coming years. But as increasing attention came my way, the time seemed right to venture out on my own. So in 1983, with Bill and Gloria's love and support, I began booking concerts on my own in churches around the country.

At first it was just my husband and me and the box of accompaniment tracks, but we gradually added others to our little entourage, including a product person and a sound technician. Best of all, as 1983 came to a close, we looked forward to an addition not just to our business but to our family.

I traveled and performed in my own concerts until I was eight months along, wearing cute little maternity outfits to hide my new, rounder shape.

I was so happy to be pregnant; I truly loved the whole experience. I couldn't believe that although God could do this baby thing without us, He chose us women to house a little life for nine months while it is growing. What an amazing blessing to be a part of that process; I felt so privileged to participate in such a miracle.

I traveled and performed in my own concerts until I was eight months along, wearing cute little maternity outfits to hide my new, rounder shape. Our sweet little angel arrived in May 1984. I was in labor two full days, but it wasn't hard labor. In fact, that was the problem: I was in labor, but nothing was happening. We had started a kids' club called the Friendship Company, and I dutifully answered all the kids' letters myself. So there I sat in my hospital bed, hooked up to the IV and writing notes to the Friendship Company kids, pausing to let the contractions pass, and waiting for our precious Anna—we pronounce her name *AHN-uh*—to make her appearance. The doctor finally decided she needed a little help, and I ended up having a Cesarean section.

Although the recovery process took a little longer than we had expected, due to the C-section, Anna and I were soon out on the road together. She was just six weeks old that summer when I accompanied Billy Graham's crusades to Amsterdam and England; since I was breast-feeding her, she went everywhere I went. When she tells people today, "I've been a road dog since day one," she really means it. She's been out there "on the road," touring with me more than anyone else in the family.

Shortly after we returned home from the crusades, we headed out on our first ever Sandi Patti (still misspelling it at that point) bus tour—in our own bus. It was organized to support my latest album with Benson, *Songs from the Heart*. In addition to the product person and sound technician, we hired a husband-and-wife team who served as bus driver and nanny, and off we went.

Busin' It

Some people think it must be awful to travel around the country on a tour bus, but I've always loved it. You get uninterrupted sleep (at least you do when you don't have an infant along), and you don't have to hassle with airports and changing planes. You go to bed, and when you wake up, you're in the concert city. It's awesome!

There are a few tricks to it, however. For instance, you want to make sure you sleep with your feet, rather than your head, toward the front of the bus, so if the driver hits the brakes in the middle of the night, you don't give yourself a concussion by banging into the headboard.

One night on the bus, one of the crew members had a nightmare. He dreamed that he was being buried alive, and in the dream he was pushing frantically on the lid of the coffin—when in reality he was pushing on the bunk above him, pinning the other crew member to the top of the bus! They both woke up screaming—and woke up all the rest of us too, of course. When we figured out what had happened, we laughed for days.

We do things a little differently today than we did back then. Usually the bus drops us off at a hotel so we can clean up, then we come back to the venue for the sound check and supper, and then we do the show, pack up the bus, and hit the road again. But back in the "olden days," we rarely had the luxury of a hotel for the day. Instead the bus drove directly to the venue, and we showered there and made it our home away from home. We set up a nursery in one of the dressing rooms, complete with baby swing, playpen, stroller, bouncing things, and all sorts of other baby apparatus. We were never ones to travel light.

I had a wonderful time with Anna during our bus-touring road-dog adventures; today I cherish those memories and wouldn't trade them for anything. But I do wish things hadn't been quite so hectic and there had been less pressure on me that this was the way things *had* to be. Her birth was the beginning of my favorite career—being a mom—and it was certainly the highlight of that year, although there were a few others, including four more Dove Awards and my first Grammy, the highest award in the music industry.

The Pressure to Perform

The Songs from the Heart Tour was continuing in spring of 1985 when Anna, being treated for a minor infection, had a severe reaction to an antibiotic containing sulfa. Our sweet little baby, not quite a year old, was hospitalized in Indianapolis for three long weeks. Yet, incredibly, we didn't cancel the tour. Looking back on that chapter of my life, it's one of my major regrets—surely my biggest failure as a mother.

The pressure on me was so great to keep the schedule intact that on those evenings when a concert was scheduled, I would fly out that morning, leaving Anna in the hospital, my parents or my husband's parents staying with her. After the concert I would rush to the airport to catch a late flight back to Indianapolis.

Every time I left Anna, I cried from the moment I kissed her good-bye until the lights dimmed in the auditorium, signaling the start of the concert. I would somehow manage to pull myself together for the show, then I would cry all the way home, both because I was worried about my baby girl and because I was racked with guilt that I had put my career ahead of my being with her constantly while she was so sick.

One night, after a concert, a woman lovingly said to me, "Honey, we're always glad to hear you sing, but you should be at that hospital with your baby." I held it together until I got into the car to go to the airport, and then I sobbed uncontrollably until I arrived in Indianapolis.

In those dark, anxious days, my prayers were often the urgent, unspoken pleadings described in Romans 8:26, which says, "The

Spirit helps us in our weakness. We do not know what we ought to pray for, but the Spirit himself intercedes for us with groans that words cannot express." I was desperate for Anna to get well and exhausted from the high-pressure demands of daily traveling, performing, and rushing back to her bedside. Weighed down by guilt and weary with worry, I sought God's presence continually, but I couldn't seem to find the words to express the terrible torment I felt.

We came close to losing Anna. To write those words makes me weep even today, more than twenty years later. It took awhile, but she finally recovered completely. I'm not sure I ever will. To this day, when I think of that worry-filled time, my conscience is plagued with self-accusations: *What kind of mother would leave her sick infant to go sing to strangers?*

It was moments like these that gave me my first glimpses of what lay ahead: a career that was spinning out of control, bringing with it equal amounts of joy and pain.

Such blessings in my life,
I ask myself if I ever thank You like I could?
In my darkest hour, love's amazing power rescues me.
—Bob Farrell and David Hamilton
"You Have Been So Good"

Chapter Four

RIDING FAME'S ROLLER COASTER

After high school my youngest brother, Craig, had followed me to Anderson, where he also attended classes at AU. A talented musician, he had an incredible ear. As our family was touring together, Dad would sometimes ask him for a note to get us started, and he would nail it every time. Just out of the blue, he could find that note. Later Craig became the number one studio tenor at Pinebrook, the Gaithers' recording facility in nearby Alexandria.

The Indiana countryside was blanketed with fog on the morning of February 17, 1986, as Craig was driving home from the studio. He topped a rise on a lonely back road and plowed into a big pileup of vehicles that had already crashed in the fog. Just twenty-four years old, Craig sustained severe head injuries and was taken by a medevac helicopter to an Indianapolis hospital.

My parents were touring on the West Coast when the accident

happened. It was my difficult duty to call them. "Mom, I hope you're sitting down," I said, "because I have some bad news."

They rushed to Indianapolis, and for the next six weeks all of us stayed at Craig's bedside as much as possible, filling the room with our loving words, prayers, and music. Trapped in a coma, he showed few signs of recovery for a long time, and eventually he was moved to a rehabilitation hospital. Occasionally he would respond to something we said or did, but those times were rare, and he did not speak. It was as though he was struggling to surface from a black, bottomless pool.

Some evenings after I had visited him in Indianapolis and gone back home, I would call Craig from Anderson; Mom would hold the phone to his ear so I could sing to him, and she would tell me afterward that tears had welled up in his eyes as he heard my voice. I always sang the same song to him: "It Is Well with My Soul." As a side note, after Craig had recovered, we were in church one day, and he mentioned to me that he loved that song. He didn't know why it was so special to him, he said, but he always cried when he heard it. We both blinked back tears as I told him that was the song I had sung to him again and again while he was in the coma. How precious to know we were connected, heart to heart, despite the darkness of that trying time.

That year, 1986, Larnelle Harris and I had been nominated for a Grammy for Best Gospel Performance for the song "I've Just Seen Jesus." It was a tremendous honor to be nominated, but I couldn't bear the thought of leaving Craig to go to the awards program, hating that once again I was faced with a choice between family and career, and also hating to picture myself in such a glamorous, party atmosphere when my brother was back home fighting for his life.

"Of course you're going," my mother told me. "What do you think Craig would want you to do? Is there any question in your mind about that?"

In the end I went. But Craig was on my mind the whole evening. I knew that one of his favorite recording groups was Mr. Mister, and when I saw that they had also been nominated for a Grammy, I started scheming to figure out how I could get an autograph for Craig from Richard Page, the group's lead singer. I hoped I might find someone who knew someone who knew Richard well enough to ask him for the favor.

Mr. Mister performed for the Grammy Awards program, and when the group members came down off the stage, I was stunned to see that they were heading for the empty seats right in front of me! During a commercial break, I leaned forward to tap Richard Page on the shoulder. I quickly explained my brother's situation and how he loved the group, and I asked if he would sign an autograph that I could take back to Craig. He graciously took my pen, jotted out a quick line, and handed it back to me with a smile.

"Mom, I hope you're sitting down," I said, *"because I have some bad news."*

I was so excited, thinking how pleased Craig would be when he came out of the coma (as I was sure he would do) and heard my story of how I got the autograph, that I almost missed the category they were announcing next. Then I heard Larnelle's name—and *my* name. At first I thought they were re-reading the list of nominees. But people were applauding and smiling at me, and I realized the truth. I couldn't believe that we had been recognized again with such an honor. Holding the Grammy in one hand and wiping away tears with the other, I dedicated the award to Craig, asking the audience for prayers on his behalf.

The gospel music categories aren't usually included in the nationally televised Grammy Awards program, but for some reason they were that night. So my request for prayers for Craig went out to an international audience. The next thing my parents knew, waiting there in Craig's hospital room, they were being inundated by phone calls from all over the world, assuring them that prayers were going up from all corners of the globe. Is it any surprise that, a few weeks later, Craig came out of the coma? Our hearts nearly burst with joy as he came back to us. How wonderful it was to see that familiar smile crease his face and to hear his voice calling our names. It would take a long time to get his life back, and even today he must deal with the injuries he received all those years ago. But his determined, arduous struggle for recovery was an inspiration to all who knew him.

A Silent Death

Craig's accident marked the beginning of a season of emotional roller-coaster rides, a time of joy and accomplishment alternating with periods of sorrow and anxiety. The Grammy lifted our spirits, and Craig's recovery sent us even higher.

Soon after that I was happy to discover I was pregnant again, and I hoped that bringing another child into the situation might help rejuvenate my marriage. But almost as soon as I celebrated the pregnancy, it ended in a miscarriage, bringing heartache instead of the joy we had anticipated. There are no more devastating words to hopeful parents-to-be than to hear a doctor say there's no sign of life in the womb.

Miscarriage is a private death, heartbreaking and grievous to the parents yet silent and invisible to everyone else. To the mom, that little child inside you is real, and the pain and sorrow you feel when the child dies can be overwhelming. But to those around you, little or nothing has changed. Maybe you don't even look different after the miscarriage, so it's hard for people to understand that you've been through a huge emotional upheaval. Those who have been through it know that miscarriage can be a lonely, painful, heartbreaking experience.

"Who Was That Singing the National Anthem?"

I was still aching from the loss of the unborn baby when the roller coaster took another sudden, unexpected swoop toward the heavens. I had recorded the national anthem for an album that was to be sold as a fund-raiser for the restoration of Ellis Island; this version included a new second verse that had been written especially for the occasion.

The Statue of Liberty had recently been restored, and the ABC television network planned a special program to broadcast the rededication ceremonies and celebrations. Roger Goodman, one of the producers of the event, suggested to the program's planners that they use my recording of the national anthem from the Ellis Island fund-raiser album. I wasn't involved in any way with the event and didn't know they were going to use it.

During that season of my life, I had some wonderful fans in the Christian community, but I wasn't really known at all in the crossover market. After they played the recording, news anchor Peter Jennings, who was hosting the program, reportedly made the comment, "That was sung by a housewife from Indiana. I'm not even sure who she is."

People began to call in to the network for one of two reasons. Either they were asking, "Who *was* that singing the national anthem?" or they were fans calling to tell Peter Jennings who I was. I have to say, this was one of the greatest performance opportunities I've ever had, and the best part was . . . I was at home the whole time! That's an artist's dream.

We were watching the program on TV like just about everyone across America. The end of the show featured a video montage of the weekend's highlights. Underscoring the beautiful images was my recording of the national anthem. To be honest, we didn't realize what it was until little Anna said, "Mommy, that's *you* singing!" I focused in to listen a moment, and sure enough, it was!

The president and first lady went home with a little part of me that night.

The next day ABC came to Anderson to do a story about the recording and the reaction to it. And there were several other interesting calls as well. One of them was from a staff member of Johnny Carson's *Tonight Show*, inviting me to come to Los Angeles and appear on the program. Johnny always loved giving new artists a moment in the spotlight, and that was how I got my first invitation to appear there.

Then came the really special invitation: the organizers of an annual charity event called Christmas in Washington asked me to be part of the huge cast of popular performers invited from all categories of the music industry. The event is held in one of the historic buildings in the capital city, and the decorators go all out to completely transform it into a spectacular display of holiday finery. It was the first time I'd done something big for a national television audience, and I was thrilled to be included. Imagine what it was like to stand up there and sing "O Holy Night!" and "Bethlehem Morning" and see President and Mrs. Reagan sitting in the front row!

Afterward I was thrilled to be introduced to the Reagans; we shook hands, and Mrs. Reagan graciously leaned forward for a little hug. As we parted, my fingernail got caught in her beaded jacket and broke off, but neither of us said anything. She probably didn't notice. I felt a little awkward, seeing the little shred of my fingernail stuck in among the beadwork as she moved on to her next guest, but it also gave me a tender thought to store away in my memory: the president and first lady went home with a little part of me that night.

The Twins

After enduring a miscarriage, it was a special blessing to learn I was pregnant with twins. Little Anna, when she heard the news, explained confidently that the baby I had lost through the miscarriage hadn't been lost at all but had simply decided to wait and come with another baby.

It seems amazing to me now to look back and think I continued touring, traveling, and singing until my sixth month of that huge pregnancy, but that's what I did. The twins were born in late November 1987, right after a couple of other twins were handed to me: a Grammy for the album *Morning Like This* and another for the song "They Say," which I had recorded with Deniece Williams. I also received three Dove Awards that year and was named *Billboard* magazine's Inspirational Artist of the Year for the second time.

But none of those honors came anywhere close to matching the joy that swept over me as Jonathan and Jennifer made their safe arrivals into this world. They were robust, healthy babies right from the start, weighing seven and eight pounds, delivered by Cesarean section. Just as they do today, they instantly brought laughter and love with them wherever they went.

The next three months of my life were some of the happiest times I had known, because for once I managed to take some time off and stay home with my family. What a pleasure it was, what a luxury, to cuddle up with Anna and the twins, to sing to them and smile as they cooed and giggled back to me. I loved being a full-time mom, loved every minute I could devote completely to being with my kids.

Sometimes I think that if I had asserted myself more and demanded more of that kind of time for myself and my family, I might not have crashed as hard as I did a few years later.

Career Demands versus Family Needs

All too soon it was time to hit the road again. There was another album to support, another tour to complete, and this time our concerts were booked in large auditoriums and arenas. A couple of years earlier we had added backup singers, a group called First Call; one of the women in that group was married to our piano player, and they had kids close to Anna's age. It was fun to see the youngsters playing backstage at the arena or sacked out in the "nursery," napping together.

But now the members of First Call were going their own way, and we had to look around for another group to sing backup. We had heard about a group called One, and when we saw them perform in a nearby town, we liked what we heard. Brent Henderson, Brian McSee, and Don Peslis had a great sound, and we felt confident they would be rewarding additions to our program, which already included some female backup singers. Dick Tunney would be coming along as musical director, and Billy Crocket was our guest artist.

> *Sometimes I think that if I had asserted myself more, I might not have crashed as hard as I did a few years later.*

Our production company, now based in a small compound of offices in Anderson, owned three tour buses and a semitruck that hauled our lighting, sound, stage, and musical equipment. Sometimes I watched the stagehands unloading the huge truck at one of the venues where we would perform and longed for the "simple" days (which we thought then were quite complicated) when Mom, Dad, my brothers, and I had traveled the country in the rented RV and brought along a stage built of plywood and cinder blocks.

Another difference in the new tour was that we were bringing along three children instead of one—although they weren't with us all the time. By then we had two nannies in our employ, and sometimes three. The husband-and-wife team had moved on, and in their place we had been helped by individual caregivers who took turns traveling and staying home as needed.

We were fortunate to have several skilled and devoted women help us as nannies over the years, but the one who's been with us the longest is Betty Fair. She and her husband, Phil, have been lifelong friends of my parents; Betty and my mom were childhood friends, and so were Phil and my dad. The Fairs had welcomed me into their home when I attended AU, and I basically adopted myself into their family. Like my parents, they have spent a lifetime serving up beautiful music to glorify God. Betty was one of the original members of the Bill Gaither Trio, and Phil has worked in music ministries at two Anderson churches while also working at Anderson University (now he is director of advancements and church relations). He was minister of music at Eastside Church of God when I attended AU, and he had hired me as the church pianist. In that role I also had become an assistant to Betty, who was the very creative director of the children's choir.

Because we had such a close relationship, it seemed perfectly natural, when my own family and career were expanding beyond our capacity to cope, to ask Betty for help. She came running to the rescue, and she's been with us ever since.

She and the other nannies made a great team in managing our family and taking care of our kids, either on the road or back at home.

As the kids got older and were able to do more things for themselves, we downsized to having only one nanny, and that one was—and still is—Betty. She is a true godsend. She's like a mom, grandma, and sister all rolled into one. Over the years she has adapted to the ever-changing dynamic of our family, and she pretty much runs our household. She's always ready with a listening ear and a little extra TLC for anyone who needs it, and there are many days when we all just line up and wait for one of her special hugs.

At the peak of my career, those devoted nannies sometimes seemed to be the one thing that stood between me and total despair. I wanted to be with my kids all the time, but that just wasn't practical. Sometimes they came along with me, but other times I left them at home. Either way I knew they would be protected and well cared for, and that gave me as much peace of mind as a mom can have when she's far away from her children.

To accommodate the twins on the tour bus when they did come along, we moved a set of bunks into the back lounge area and installed two gates that completely closed off both bunks. Their bunks were on the driver's side of the bus, and I slept on a couch on the other side with a narrow walkway between us. At bedtime or when they awoke in the morning, they looked like two little puppies in a pet store, peering out through the grid to smile at me.

Whenever I had to be gone for a long time, maybe ten days or so, we would divide up the time so the kids came with me for a while; then when we had a day off, we would take them home and leave them with Betty or one of the other nannies for the rest of the tour. I don't think I was away from them for more than five days at a time or maybe a week, at the longest.

The Peak

Audiences were responding warmly to our concerts, and it seemed God was continuing to open doors to remarkable opportunities. I was becoming accustomed to standing on a stage confidently and happily performing before audiences of thousands of people. But the image wasn't a true reflection of what was happening behind the scenes. Sometimes I felt like I was being swallowed up by my career. And I couldn't run home at the end of a performance to pour out my heart and vent my emotions because my home life and my business had become interwoven into one all-encompassing tapestry: beautiful and orderly on the surface, a tangle of knots underneath.

I was beginning to feel trapped. I pictured myself as one of those cartoon characters who gets covered with snow and then trips, starts rolling down a hill, and turns into a snowball. The snowball grows larger and larger and rolls faster and faster until, inevitably, it runs up against one rock too many and is shattered into a million pieces. I was on a roll, and while my career was skyrocketing, my marriage was on a collision course with disaster.

My home life and my business had become interwoven into one all-encompassing tapestry: beautiful and orderly on the surface, a tangle of knots underneath.

There were times, after a successful concert had ended and the arena was still echoing with the cheers of the crowd, when I was huddled in a corner of my dressing room, sobbing in misery. But it felt like there was no way out, nothing to do but get back on the bus and ride on to the next city, where it would probably all play out again in the same sad, unavoidable scenario.

The bright spot in this time of gathering gloom was my kids. Having them with me was, and still is, the greatest joy of my life. Now that we were performing in large arenas, they were discovering the fun of bathing and playing in the huge showers in the sports teams' locker rooms. We would get some plastic cups from the caterers and turn on all the showerheads, and they would run around in there, throwing water on each other and having a blast. It was so funny to see these little-bitty naked kids splashing and playing and laughing in the water.

Anna was our little twinkle-toes dancer. She started taking dance lessons at age three, and she loved to twirl and whirl around the backstage areas of the arenas and auditoriums, pretending to give her own enthralling dance recitals. She was very creative in how she filled her time at the venue. On one tour we bought her a pair of roller skates, and one of the backup singers carefully coached her until she was zooming all over the place, zipping in and out of the cavernous lower-level hallways of the arena.

Another Accident

Back home for a few days in November 1989, my husband and I slipped out for an anniversary dinner, taking every opportunity we could to reconnect and attempt to relight the fire of passion in our marriage. We left the kids with one of our regular nannies and headed for a local restaurant. We had a cell phone, but if you were around in 1989, you know that cell phones back then were a lot different than they are today. While today's models may weigh a few ounces and be small enough to fit in your pocket, those early models weighed a few *pounds* and fit inside a small tote bag. So we left the cell phone in the car, and when we called home as soon as we'd finished dinner, our *other* nanny answered the phone. There had been an accident, she said, and little Jonathan, then an almost-two-year-old live wire, had accidentally pulled over the sturdy wooden hall tree that stood beside our front door. It was one of those tall hat racks with big metal hooks standing out from the center post, and one of the hooks had hit Jonathan in the head.

The first nanny had hurriedly called the second nanny to come stay with Anna and Jennifer while she drove Jonathan to the emergency room. By the time we got home, they were back. The cut didn't look too bad; the doctor had just shaved away a little bit of his curly red hair, cleaned the wound, put in a few sutures, and sent him back home. We were relieved that it seemed like a minor incident.

But the next morning, Jonathan's face was badly swollen, and even worse, the left side of his little body was paralyzed. We rushed him back to the local ER, where doctors did a CAT scan and found hemorrhaging in Jonathan's brain. The metal hook of the hall tree had fractured his skull and pushed the broken segments of bone inward, piercing the brain tissue.

The next thing I knew, we were at Methodist Hospital in Indianapolis, where an emergency neurological team had been summoned to perform brain surgery on my precious little boy. Listening to the doctor explain the delicate procedure was almost more than I could bear. They would have to find and remove the broken shards of the skull, stop the hemorrhaging, drain the blood, and do their best to repair any damage.

I was on the verge of collapse that day as I gently handed Jonathan over to the nurse, not knowing whether I would ever see him alive again. Weeping uncontrollably as the doors to the surgical suite swung shut behind him, I sank into a chair beside my husband, and together we begged God to spare our son. A few minutes later, the doors to the operating room swung open again and one of the nurses emerged, carrying an envelope. "We thought you might like to have this," she said, gently placing the envelope in my hands.

Inside were the beautiful red curls of Jonathan's hair.

The next few days were long and full of prayer as we anxiously watched Jonathan for signs of brain damage and/or recuperation. We were thankful for tiny indications of improvement here and there, but he was obviously a long way from recovery. We didn't know what the future held for him. Doctors had had to remove small bits of brain tissue that were irreparably damaged, and they told us that, unlike some organs in the body, brain tissue does not regenerate. What was gone was gone forever, and we didn't know what that would mean for Jonathan.

He wasn't making much progress; he rarely spoke and was mostly lethargic all day, every day. Then "Grandma Doris" (my husband's mother) brought Jonathan's twin sister, Jenni, to the hospital for a visit. He spotted her as they were wheeling her down the hallway in her stroller, and all of a sudden he burst into excited jibber-jabbering like nothing we'd ever heard before! They chatted away in their own private little conversation, and with that Jonathan turned a corner and was soon gaining back a lot of the physical and mental capabilities he had lost.

The effects of the accident are still with him, however. He's had to work hard to overcome some learning disabilities, and he enjoys keeping to himself. But his shy demeanor hides a huge amount of talent. I'll tell you about it later, in chapter 11.

Understanding Past Hurts

As I watched my children growing from infants to toddlers to happy, exuberant youngsters, a nightmarish memory kept seeping into my mind from my own otherwise happy childhood. I had never told anyone about the incident. It happened when I was quite young and my parents had left me with a trusted baby-sitter for a few days while they were traveling with one of the music groups.

It had been a very unpleasant episode in my life, but like most children who've been sexually abused, I thought I must have done something bad to deserve that kind of treatment; after all, as a child I believed that adults don't do bad things to children. What this woman had done seemed wrong, but it must *not* have been wrong, I reasoned in my childish thinking, because the baby-sitter was an adult, and adults don't do bad things. And since I believed I somehow deserved what she did to me, I thought if I told my parents about what had happened, they would see that I'd done something bad, and they might even punish me for whatever unknown thing that was.

None of this makes sense if you're an adult, of course—especially if you're an adult who's never experienced any kind of abuse. But as this memory repeatedly leaked into my adult psyche, I started tossing it around in my mind, looking at it from different perspectives. Suddenly one sharp thought penetrated through all the other misconceptions: *I would* never *want anyone to do that to any of my children!* And if that was the case, then my parents probably hadn't wanted anyone to do it to their child either. Finally, the facts were falling into place: The thing that had been done to me was wrong. Totally, absolutely, inexcusably wrong.

I had never told anyone else what happened to me. But one day I felt brave enough to share it with a dear friend who had become my mentor in Bible Study Fellowship. "I don't know if this is anything I need to deal with," I told her, "but it's just been on my mind a lot lately."

Wonderful woman that she is, she validated my concerns, wrapped me in her arms, and said, "Sandi, it absolutely is something you need to deal with." She gave me a book by Lana Bateman, *God's Crippled Children.*[1]

Like most children who've been sexually abused, I thought I must have done something bad to deserve that kind of treatment.

I read that book and thought of a dozen people who really needed to read it. Then, after I'd finished reading it, it was as if the Lord was saying to me, *It's not for someone else. It's for you, Sandi. Read it again.*

So I read through it again, all the way, and I realized that so many problems in my life—weight issues, boundary issues, poor-relationship issues, and a host of other things—could be traced back to the ramifications of that childhood abuse. I wasn't reading the book thinking, *That could be me.* I was reading it and realizing, *Wow! That IS me!*

I went back to my mentoring friend and said, "I don't really know if any of this relates to what happened, but could I just process some of it out loud to you? Here are the thoughts that came to me as I read through the book, and I'm asking the Lord to just lead me through this process." I told her how the baby-sitter had seemed sweet and kind as my parents dropped me off that day, but as soon as their car disappeared from the driveway, her demeanor turned cold and harsh. "Go put your things away," she said, a hard bitterness edging her voice.

At bedtime she gave me milk and cookies, but there was no warmth in her gesture. I had brought along my favorite night-gown, but when she saw it she fumed, "Why would you want to wear that ugly thing? Here, put this on." She handed me a long, white nightgown, watched as I put it on, then put me to bed and turned out the light.

She slept in a second bed in the same room, and sometime later in the night, I awoke to find myself lying on my back, naked, the covers pulled back, and the baby-sitter standing over me, washing my genital area with a washcloth in a mechanical sort of back-and-forth motion. This was repeated every night that I stayed with the woman. I was the focus of a bizarre ritual in which I was touched in a way that did not cause physical pain but traumatized me nonetheless. I was confused by what was happening, but I was too scared to open my eyes and tell her to stop. Each night I pretended to sleep through it. During the day the baby-sitter was cold and distant but provided for my needs.

When my parents picked me up a few days later, I climbed into the car, happy to see them, and never mentioned what had happened. "It was just that one thing, that one confusing experi-ence," I told my friend. "I wasn't physically hurt, really; she didn't even touch my skin. She rubbed me with a washcloth. It wasn't like I was raped or anything. But somehow I just can't let it go."

My friend assured me that such instances could, indeed, have an impact on adult life. She helped me contact Lana Bateman, who invited me to Dallas to meet with a counselor there. With his help I pulled the buried story into the light, pieced it together, and came to understand that the baby-sitter had violated my trust in adults, and she had also violated me, both physically and emotionally.

An experience while we were out on the road helped me understand the impact of that event on my life. One morning one of the backup singers came rushing down to breakfast in the hotel, and he seemed totally confused to find the rest of us there. He couldn't figure out why people were eating breakfast; he thought breakfast should have been over.

The clock in his room had been set wrong. It was two hours off, but he hadn't realized it. He had simply trusted the clock to show the right time. So when he awoke, he was shocked to see how late it was. He thought, *I never sleep this late. Something must be wrong with me.* But then he turned on the TV and was puzzled to see that the *Today* show was still on. *What is going on?* he wondered.

Still not figuring out what had happened, he hurried down to the lobby, expecting everyone to have already left for the venue, and instead there we sat, eating a leisurely breakfast.

He continued to flit around the room, insisting that we should be leaving and asking why everyone was just sitting around. Finally someone asked him, "What time do you think it is?"

He said, "It's eleven o'clock. Why are we still here?"

"It's not eleven. It's nine," the other crew member replied.

Finally, when he had the truth, everything else made sense.

A similar thing happens when you've been sexually abused.

You're basing all your information on a couple of facts that are not right: (1) adults don't do bad things to children, so (2) I must have done something terrible to deserve that treatment.

When you start dealing with that abuse and, in my case, getting help from professional therapists, you reset that clock. You learn the truth, and you also learn that you do have choices when, before, you might have believed you shouldn't question others' behavior toward you or authority over you.

The more progress I made through professional therapy, the more some previously puzzling things made sense. For example, even though I grew up in a totally supportive environment, with the most loving and nurturing parents anyone could ever have, I still subconsciously thought of myself as damaged goods. Mom

I had the self-esteem of an old, tattered and stained rag doll with one eye missing.

and Dad never, ever gave me messages, spoken or unspoken, that told me I was anything but the most precious daughter in the world, yet deep inside I had the self-esteem of an old, tattered and stained rag doll with one eye missing. In therapy I came to understand that this is a common way of thinking among those who have suffered abuse. We feel this way, but we don't know why. Sometimes we have to have professional help to reframe our self-image.

Later, after I returned from spending two weeks in a residential counseling center, there was a night when one of my kids—I can't even remember which one—brought home a library book for us to read together. We cuddled up in a chair, and I read aloud Margery Williams's classic tale of *The Velveteen Rabbit*. It is the story of a toy rabbit who started out being "fat and bunchy, as a rabbit should be;

his coat was spotted brown and white, he had real thread whiskers, and his ears were lined with pink sateen." He was a Christmas present to a little boy, who fell in love with the rabbit. Being the boy's constant companion made the rabbit happy—so happy, in fact, that he didn't notice how "his beautiful velveteen fur was getting shabbier and shabbier, and his tail coming unsewn, and all the pink rubbed off his nose where the Boy had kissed him."

One day when he was still new he had asked another toy in the nursery, the Skin Horse, what it meant to be real. The wise horse replied, "When a child loves you for a long, long time, not just to play with, but REALLY loves you, then you become Real. . . . Generally, by the time you are Real, most of your hair has been loved off, and your eyes drop out and you get loose in the joints and very shabby. But these things don't matter at all, because once you are Real you can't be ugly, except to people who don't understand."

Reading those words, my eyes filled with tears. I thought, *Inside, I may feel tattered and stained, and my fur's been loved off, but I'm real.* For the first time I understood what it was like to feel really loved by God—not because of what I could *do* for Him or how high I could sing songs for Him but simply because He just loved me. That is the key to becoming real. Suddenly my negative image of myself as a raggedy old doll was reframed. Yes, I might be emotionally scarred, but I was real now (or at least more real than I had ever been). I had value, and I was loved. At last I could accept all those precious facts about myself. What a sweet moment that was, even as my little one was asking, "Why are you crying, Mommy?"

In therapy I gained more insight into how the childhood abuse had spilled over into some of my other adult behaviors and feelings. As the therapist helped me revisit my memories about the abusive baby-sitter, I came to see that the nightly gift of chocolate-chip cookies and milk was the only bit of sanity and comfort in the craziness of that emotionally hurtful environment. And still today, when I feel stressed out or emotionally pressured, I find myself in the kitchen stirring up a batch of chocolate-chip cookies, even though I now recognize the negative source of this crazy urge. Needing something I can enjoy and control, I turn to food for comfort from present-day stresses (sometimes while thinking, *Here's an eating disorder waiting to happen!*).

I know there can be a wide range of opinions when it comes to childhood-abuse issues and how they impact adult life. It's my opinion that most of the people who have a hard time understanding these issues were most likely never abused or traumatized as children. My own belief is that I can't press on toward the goal God has set for me until I'm at peace with what has come before. That doesn't mean I want to dwell on the past; getting hung up on what happened to me all those years ago means I'm still a victim. The victory over those troubles has come for me as I've gained understanding and perspective about what happened and, most importantly, as I've realized that I can choose to set those issues aside.

Learning that I have a choice, that I can say no, and that I can assert my own feelings and opinions, has been a huge step forward for me.

Unfortunately, some of the choices I was about to make would cause even more unpleasant and painful consequences for me—and for a lot of other people.

You left the ninety and nine
To save the one lost sheep.
Good shepherd, You came looking for me.
—Bob Farrell and Greg Nelson
"Savior Came (When I Was Needy)"

Chapter Five

THE PINNACLE OF SUCCESS, THE DEPTHS OF DESPAIR

Others come away from a visit to the presidential retreat at Camp David with a sense of awe and gratitude. I came home with those sentiments too—plus a broken ankle. In 1991, a few months after the conclusion of the Gulf War, my family was invited to join President George Herbert Walker Bush, his wife, Barbara, and the families of the Joint Chiefs of Staff at Camp David for a weekend of worship and thanksgiving. I had been asked to lead one of the services and to do a little story-time program for the children who were there, including my own. My parents and I sang, and at the end of the second evening, we joined the rest of the guests for a delicious barbecue. Then some of us started a killer game of wallyball, which, for the uninformed, is volleyball played on a court with walls.

We were having a blast, and I was showing off my athletic

prowess for the president (I had been a competitive volleyball player in high school) when I went up to block a shot—and came down wrong and twisted my ankle.

Although it was painful, it certainly wasn't an emergency, so the president's physician wrapped it tightly in an Ace bandage and suggested I have it x-rayed when I got back home. He found a set of crutches for me, and I hobbled off to the airport, eager to tell anyone who asked what had happened—and where!

The incident sort of illustrated the way things were going for me in that season of my life. I was enjoying so many blessings I couldn't begin to count them all. By the end of that year I had won a total of twenty-eight Dove Awards (including the award for Female Vocalist of the Year for ten straight years) and five Grammys. I had four beautiful children (sweet little Erin had arrived the previous year) and a schedule packed full of performance dates. Yet at the same time, something in my life was broken. In the depths of my heart, I often felt like the most miserable person on earth, a lost lamb stumbling away from the Shepherd's fold.

Although things had slowed down a little in 1990, I knew the Sandi Patti caravan (I was still misspelling it) would soon be gearing up to resume its "normal" endurance run around the country. During the peak of my career, I was doing as many as two hundred concerts a year, averaging four a week, while trying to be the devoted mother of four young children and, with what meager amount of energy I had left, a good wife. Maybe some other twentieth-century superwoman might have pulled it off, but I was hovering on the brink of a breakdown.

The pressure was relentless. Not only was I the sole support for my family, I was also the source of income for a growing company of twenty-five employees. The business became the constant topic of conversation whether I was at home, in the office, or touring. There was so little time for being a wife and mother. So little time for happiness. Gradually it seemed that the only common interests my husband and I shared were the four children and the business, which was my voice and all it entailed. Rarely were any other topics discussed.

I couldn't afford to get sick, yet I felt sick a great deal of the time, probably due to stress. But too much was at stake; too many people were counting on me. I wasn't allowed to take any more time off—at least that's how it seemed to me.

I had benefited greatly from the therapy I'd sought for the issues surrounding my childhood abuse. Having seen the rewards of professional counseling, I attended a presentation at our church featuring a popular local marriage counselor. His message was full of hope, encouragement, and promise; I loved what he had to say, and soon my husband and I began a series of sessions with the counselor that helped us understand the differences that were pushing us apart. Much of the problem lay in the fact that I had changed the playing field. I had learned that I had a right to express some of my own opinions and make some choices, and occasionally my choices threw a wrench in the workings of the company that previously had seemed to operate so smoothly. For example, as the mother of four young children, I wanted to be home more, even if that meant fewer concerts and less income.

Not only was I the sole support for my family, I was also the source of income for a growing company of twenty-five employees.

I was rocking the boat, creating tension, but I could see only one way out of the deteriorating situation. In one of our last sessions together with the counselor, I said I thought it would be best if we separated our marriage from our business. I was suggesting that my husband step down as my manager. Reluctantly, he agreed to do so.

Changes

It was a difficult, painful time, and just as I was responsible for supporting all the other people linked to my career, I was also responsible for the anguish the next few months would bring to all of them. But I believed that ultimately it would be what was best for everyone.

A few more months went by, and I took another upsetting step, separating from my husband. At first I moved in with my parents, who also made room for the kids to be there when it was my turn to have them. Then I bought a big old house in town, close to the kids' school.

The press would say later, when I filed for divorce in 1992, that I "gave no reasons" for the dissolution of our fourteen-year marriage. There were reasons, of course. But the fact was that while I was divorcing my husband, he remained the beloved father of my children, and given the pain I was already causing them by initiating the breakup, I wasn't going to bring further distress to them by publicly airing the intimate details of our failed marriage. I made a decision then that I would seek always to honor my children's father, and I continue to hold to that decision today.

The next few years would be the most difficult time of my life, a season of mental anguish, guilt, emotional pain, and depression.

In telling my story in this book, I know that sharing more details from that time would give you, the reader, a clearer picture of the struggles I went through, the grieving and the emotional stress as well as the extensive counseling that surrounded the end of our marriage. I want to be as honest and open as I possibly can because I want you to see that, for Christians, divorce is never the easy way out. I also want to show you how, even in the depths of the greatest pain and the darkest days imaginable, God can find you and bring healing to your life.

But I cannot share all the facts of my situation while holding to my commitment to honor my children's father. I do not mean to gloss over this part of my story and make it seem like an easy turning point in my life. It absolutely was not. But it was a time of personal conversations and dozens of counseling sessions, and those exchanges must, for the most part, remain private.

The Hardest Day

My husband and I did our best to reduce the pain our separation would cause the kids. But Anna, our oldest child, who's now a beautiful young woman of twenty, was bright enough to notice that something was wrong.

"Mom was leaving to do a Billy Graham Crusade in Argentina, and she had decided to take my sister Jenni and me," she told an interviewer. "When she was getting us ready to leave, I thought it was strange that Dad wasn't going. We had gone on a similar trip to Japan the year before, and he had gone with us. I wondered why Dad wasn't going with us now. Then, as we left, they just gave each other a hug and kind of a little side kiss. I was just a second-grader at that time, but second-graders can be very perceptive. I remember thinking, *That's not natural.*

"And something else unusual happened when we came back home. Mom knocked on the door before she opened it. I thought that was odd," Anna said.

I share Anna's recollections here because she is quick to share them herself. All the kids are very open about their feelings concerning what happened; I think they've found that talking about the experience has brought healing. They're also quick to reach out to friends whose parents are going through a divorce, encouraging them to share what's going on in their heads and in their hearts.

My husband and I agreed to share custody and made arrangements for my things to be moved to the old house I'd bought at a time when the moving would be the least noticeable to the kids, who were about seven, four, and two at the time. When everything was in place, we called Anna in first to break the news.

> *I wished desperately that there was some other way to survive the impossible situation. But there wasn't.*

"They sat me down and explained to me that things had changed between the two of them," she told the interviewer. "They said they don't think it's going to be for the best if they live together anymore. They said it had nothing to do with us kids, that they still loved us so much, and they continued to try to reinforce that.

"I never cried," Anna said. "Never cried the whole time. I was older and had a different perspective on things than the other kids. I had spent more time on the road with them. I saw my parents' relationship for what it really was, not for what it was supposed to be. So I really got it. And I also had a clearer understanding than the younger kids did of what it meant for Mom and Dad to separate."

We had been living out in a rural area, and the house I had bought was just down the street from some of Anna's school friends. At first she seemed more excited about moving into town than she was upset about the fact that her parents were separating.

As a toddler, Erin was too young to understand what was happening. But the four-year-old twins needed to be told. As gently and simply as possible, we laid out the situation for them. Jonathan was quiet and didn't say much. But Jenni's face was oh, so sad, and the biggest tear welled up in her eye and ran slowly down her soft little cheek. Jenni was a daddy's girl through and through, and the thought of being away from him broke her heart. In my memory I can see that tear rolling slowly down her cheek even today, and it causes me as much remorse now as it did back then. It's an awful thing to cause your children to be hurt, and I wished desperately that there was some other way to survive the impossible situation. But there wasn't. And now the die was cast.

Crossing the Line

The first few dates back out on the road seemed quieter and more relaxed as the artists and crew adjusted to the new organization. We spent a lot of time talking and laughing together.

For a long time, Don Peslis, one of the backup singers, and I had been friends and nothing more. But now I found myself looking for ways to spend more and more time with him, still doing nothing more than talking. I was treading on dangerous ground.

I know that now, and I wish I had made different choices in the next few months. But I was starving for kindness and caring attention, and Don offered it to me in his thoughtful and gracious way. I was drawn to him like water to a sponge.

Before much longer we had crossed the moral line. Instead of being just friends, we became intimately involved.

I make no excuses for what happened. It was my fault. I made a terrible mistake, falling in love with one man while I was still married to another. Don was also married. So our mistake would cause tremendous misery for both our families. There would be a huge price to pay over the next four years as I struggled through the steps of seeking forgiveness for what I had done and being restored to wholeness.

Lies and Damage Control

When I filed for divorce in early 1992, the event made headlines in the local newspapers and was reported in the national press. At the time some people said to me, "You're taking the easy way out. You think if you're in a situation you don't like, you can just quit."

They have no idea! There's nothing easy about divorce. The *easiest* thing would have been to just let everything go back to the way it had been. In the short run, that would have caused less pain for everyone else, especially my children. And believe me, the hardest thing in the world is to see your kids hurt and to know there just is no other option than to keep on going in that painful direction toward wholeness. What happens is, once you're far enough along in your journey toward emotional healing, you just can't turn back. You've suddenly had this glimpse of a healthy future, you've been given a gift of hope, and you can't turn back once you have it in your sights.

I was doing what I believed I had to do. But I'm sure, seeing the headlines, secular readers must have thought, *Another Christian celebrity turns out to be a hypocrite.* It was a difficult time for me, seeing how many people I had let down, how much damage I had done to the cause of Christ. I had let myself be portrayed as a sweet, submissive wife who used her voice to proclaim the glory and goodness of God. Now all the world knew was that I was abandoning my marriage and giving no reasons—biblical or otherwise.

And then there was that terrible secret hovering out there, the adulterous affair, which had the potential to tarnish, if not destroy, everything I had accomplished. As the months passed, a few rumors had trickled out, and the pressure to maintain the secret increased. But most of the pressures at that time concerned only the impending divorce and the way it had disappointed (and angered) many of my fans. Many churches and other venues had canceled concert dates, some radio stations had pulled my music from their play lists, and I knew it was only a matter of time before record sales started to drop.

In addition to all of my other worries, I was also in the midst of the emotional task of laying off most of the employees of the business. As I had gotten more involved in the company's dealings, I had been forced to reevaluate its focus. Suddenly I was asking myself just what my priorities were: Was I a bus company? No. A publisher? No. A management company? No. Yet the business included all those components, even though most of those services were also provided by my record label or my booking agency. We were unnecessarily duplicating a multitude of tasks, and the smartest solution was obviously to downsize. But doing so meant I would have to let go all the wonderful, fantastic employees who had become like (or were) family members.

I couldn't do it without help, so I decided on two people who would be retained to serve as my assistant and my business manager. Then the three of us set about breaking the news to the others. It was the most awkward of days as, all morning, I sat in my office and called one telephone extension after another, asking sweetly, "Uh, could you come back and talk to me for a minute?"

Everyone knew what was coming, of course. But that only made it harder. Although most of the employees understood why I was taking these steps, there were some anguished tears sprinkled throughout the day.

My emotional state at that point was off the distress scale, but I managed to put up a facade for the music industry. As news of the divorce spread, some of my peers, business associates, and charity-organization colleagues called and asked questions, either directly or circumspectly. There had been some talk, they said, probably just rumors, and they needed to know whether the rumors were true.

They wanted to know if I was having an affair.

"Absolutely not," I insisted. "No way."

It was a lie.

A New Beginning

I found myself in a stage of life I had never expected and certainly never prepared for. Professionally, I had been at the top of my game in 1992. Each year for the last decade I had won the

Dove Award for Female Vocalist of the Year; for five years I'd also received the highest award of all, Artist of the Year. I had been performing in huge arenas, and record sales had been good, with five gold albums and two platinum. I seemed to have everything going for me—except that my personal life was in shambles.

Now, as the pressures mounted from within and without, I abruptly decided to cancel the remaining dates in the current tour, Another Time, Another Place. It was a big, unfortunate step; entertainers have to be dependable if they want to get bookings in the future. But I was beginning to wonder whether I even had a future as an entertainer. In 1993, for the first time in eleven years, I didn't win a single Dove Award.

Throughout that chapter of my life, when turmoil and sin were in full swing, I continued going to church. On Sunday you would find me sitting there in Park Place Church of God, the same church I had attended for years, the church where I had been married, my children sitting beside me (when it was my turn to have them). Of course one of the reasons I was there was for the kids. I had grown up in church, just as they were doing, and I wanted to continue that tradition. My parents had given me an incredibly strong foundation of faith, and I wanted to hand down that gift to my children. It was important. But it was more than a gift to be handed down. It was a continuing gift for me as well. I needed God's constant presence in my life, even though I knew some of my choices weren't in line with His will.

They wanted to know if I was having an affair. "Absolutely not," I insisted. "No way." It was a lie.

I loved God and cherished His Word. Yes, I was straying from

His teachings, but I wanted to keep His truth in front of me. I wanted to be confronted by it regularly so I wouldn't become numb to the sin I was committing, thinking no one was noticing and thus that I was getting away with it. Maybe this sounds like crazy logic, but it's honestly how I felt during that time.

I suppose I was also there as a show of defiance. I knew I was the topic of lots of rumors and gossip throughout the community, and I was determined that no matter what people said about me, I was going to be there in public on Sunday with the attitude, *You can think what you want, but you're going to think it facing me. We're going to deal with this.*

So I was continuing my lifelong custom of attending church. But at the same time, I was looking for a new beginning. One Sunday when it was my turn to have the kids, I loaded them into the car and drove to North Anderson Church of God. After dropping off the kids in Sunday school, I happened onto the door leading to the balcony. Without really thinking about it, I started up the stairs. Soon I found myself on the top row in the back, sitting under the hues of color washing down from the huge stained-glass window above me.

As soon as I settled onto the pew, all the pent-up emotions of the last few weeks seemed to rush through me, and I quietly began to sob. There was a baby dedication that day, and I was touched by the way it was done. The parents brought the baby up to the pastor, and he began by asking them to affirm their relationship with Christ. Then he asked them to affirm their relationship with each other. Seeing the parents turn to each other and make that commitment, I realized I would not be able to do the same thing for my own children, and the thought broke my heart all over again, knowing the kids would not have both parents there, together, as they grew up. Then my mind inexplicably raced ahead to weddings, and I found myself musing about who would sit where as our children exchanged their wedding vows. With all these thoughts and images swirling through my head, I was consumed by sadness, sarcastically scolding myself, *What a great "new beginning" this is!*

Still, it felt good to let the tears flow. I knew I had an hour or so to cry, and then I would have to pull myself together and put my happy face back on so I could pick up the kids and go home.

As the service ended, the pastor came down from the pulpit and took a few steps down one of the aisles of the large, airy sanctuary.

"If you're visiting with us today, we're so glad you're here," he said. *Oh, please don't make the visitors stand up,* I prayed, trying to find a dry tissue and hoping my mascara had not slid down to my chin.

But the pastor continued, "There are people all around you who would like to know your name, if you would like to tell them," he offered. And then he added, "We want you to know that the God we serve lives within these walls—and outside these walls too."

He took a few more steps down the aisle and looked all around the crowd. "But maybe you've been visiting with us here this morning, and you're not ready to tell anyone your name. Maybe all you want to do is sit on the back row of the balcony and cry. That's OK," he said. "We want you to know that the God we serve knows how to find you there. He hasn't forgotten about you. We serve the God of second chances, of new beginnings. We serve the

God who sets His children free."

I was shocked that his words seemed aimed directly at me, although the pastor, Jim Lyon, would tell me later that he had not seen me there, broken, on the back row of the balcony. But most of all, I was given another glimpse of hope, and it meant the world to me that day. Without even knowing it, Pastor Lyon was acknowledging my presence and validating my feelings. That was probably the single biggest thing anyone could have done for me in that messy time of my life.

He wasn't telling me, "Pull it together. Pray more. Suck it up."

He wasn't saying, "You don't have a right to feel this way. God is victory."

He was simply saying, "If you just want to sit on the back row and cry, it's OK."

Finding Sanctuary

Since that morning thirteen years ago, I've lived out the idea that a church should not only *have* a sanctuary, it should *be* a sanctuary. That's what North Anderson Church of God became for me.

In olden times, a sanctuary was a place where a weary warrior or traveler could go for rest and care. In that place, nobody asked a lot of questions; instead the caregivers provided water and food and a place to rest. They bound up the wounds of the visitor so he could go back out and continue his journey or return to battle.

That's how I felt in that church. The pastor and the congregation provided a sanctuary where I could rest and recuperate, and where my emotional wounds could be healed. The people there weren't in my face all the time, confronting me. Instead they provided a place where God could confront me—and where I could confront myself. Then they guided me through the steps of restoration and encouraged me as I stepped out of that safe place and resumed my journey.

In the old rugged cross, stained with blood so divine,
A wondrous beauty I see;
For 'twas on that old cross Jesus suffered and died
To pardon and sanctify me.
—George Bennard
"The Old Rugged Cross"

HEADING FOR CALVARY . . . BY WAY OF CLEVELAND

Taking advantage of a single day off from co-hosting the Young Messiah Tour in November 1994, I had hurriedly made arrangements to fly home for the twins' birthday. I wouldn't actually get to be there on the big day, but it was the best I could do, and I was eager to celebrate early with them. Their dad and I had worked out a schedule so they stayed with him when I was on the road.

I rushed to catch the airplane, planning to take a connecting flight out of Cleveland and be home in time for the twins' bedtime. Then I would have most of the next day to spend with them before taking another late flight to catch up with the tour that night.

An early winter storm arrived in Cleveland at the same time I did, and it seemed that the moment my plane touched down, the airport closed up. The terminal was soon a crowded scene of stranded travelers, fussy babies, cranky employees, and at least one very distraught mother: me. I wasn't going to make it home. The next day's flight from Cleveland to Indianapolis, if it was able to go at all, would get in so late that there would be no time to make the one-hour drive to Anderson, see the kids, and then drive back to the airport in time for the return flight.

There was nothing left to do but cry, so I curled up on the floor in one of the gate areas, turned my back to the teeming masses, and did just that. I had heard the disappointment in the kids' voices when I called home to say I wasn't coming after all. "When *are* you coming, Mommy?" one of the twins had asked.

I had no answer. I didn't even know when our next day off from the tour would be.

As the long evening passed, my depression grew. Instead of crying about not getting home for the twins' birthday, I was crying about everything. It was as though I were back in the church balcony, but instead of feeling the relief from tension my tears had brought that Sunday morning, I was consumed with guilt and grief and loss, and there was no relief in sight. It seemed I had been crying for a year, maybe more. I cried every chance I got, every time I stepped out of the spotlight and left the cheering crowds behind.

> I curled up on the floor in one of the gate areas, turned my back to the teeming masses, and cried.

My life was a wreck. I felt like a failure as a mother because I was away from my kids more than I wanted to be. I had certainly been a failure as a wife. I was a failure as a Christian—and a hypocrite, to boot. The news of my divorce, finalized in 1993, had already caused a lot of consternation in the Christian world, and my career had felt that impact. No longer was I the darling of gospel music, reaping praise and applause wherever I went. The fans were starting to see another side of me, and while many of them understood that even Christian marriages fail, others held me to a higher standard and were hurt and disillusioned to think a Christian celebrity would take such a drastic step.

I had also taken another step that impacted my career. I had wanted to do it for a long time but had never had the courage and confidence to make the choice. But in 1994 I did it: I corrected the spelling of my last name, changing it back to Patty.

I didn't think changing my name back to its correct spelling would be a big deal. My parents were Ron and Carolyn Patty, my brothers were Michael and Craig Patty, and I was Sandi Patty. After fifteen years and sixteen albums, I wanted my name back. It was just one little letter, for heaven's sake. I didn't see why anyone would care.

My current and past record labels cared, and the press reported it as though it were some big announcement. But I felt good that in one area of my life I could easily correct a mistake.

The Long Road Back toward Restoration

After becoming a member of the North Anderson Church of God, I had met occasionally for individual counseling with Pastor Lyon and had been helped by his straight talk and insightful guidance. The congregation had been very welcoming to me, and hoping to repay a small portion of their kindness, I had scheduled a concert at the church in fall 1993 to coincide with the release of a new album, *Le Voyage*.

A few days before the concert, however, two people made an appointment with Pastor Lyon, deeply troubled that the church would host a concert by someone who, they said, was having an affair. They were responsible members of another church family, not North Anderson's, but they offered no proof of their charges, only hearsay.

Pastor Lyon suggested that they contact me directly with the charges, but they refused, and they also would not let Pastor Lyon use their names in discussing the issue with me. So the concert went on as planned.

Shortly afterward my ex-husband and his pastor from Park Side Church of God began to meet in counseling sessions with Pastor Lyon and me. The divorce was final, but the pain and bitterness were ongoing, and all of us wanted to find a way to bring peace and healing to the situation, for our sake as well as our children's.

At the first session, my ex-husband laid out a list of grievances that were still causing him pain. One of them was that I had been involved in adultery while I was married to him and that my affair with Don Peslis was continuing.

In front of my ex-husband and the two pastors, I acknowledged the truth of what he was saying. For the first time, I admitted aloud to the affair.

In our next meeting, I presented my own list of grievances.

These pastoral counseling sessions would continue for the next year or more as John and I struggled, with the pastors' help, to find a way to continue relating, despite the divorce, so we could function cooperatively as parents to love, protect, and care for our children. None of the sessions were easy; in between the appointments, I worried and grieved and prayed, asking God for strength to hang on.

At one point Pastor Lyon told me that Don and I needed to break off contact. In fact, he told me that I needed to behave "as though Don were dead." He didn't say this had to be a permanent thing; on the other hand, he didn't say it was temporary either. The grief I felt, added to the other emotions that filled my head and my heart, was almost overwhelming.

At the same time, I knew the big, bad secret about our adulterous affair would inevitably become public, and when it did, I could face an end to my career in the Christian music industry. I had learned that a freelance reporter was preparing an article about me, including information about the divorce and probably about the affair. He had been making phone calls and asking questions, and I knew it wouldn't take long before he pieced the puzzle together. I didn't know when the story would run, but it was glowing menacingly out there beyond my reach like a bucket of red-hot coals. I knew that when it was published, it would unleash a firestorm.

I kept thinking if I could do the right thing, maybe I could keep holding off the release of the article. But if I did the wrong thing, I knew it would be published as quickly as possible. But what was the wrong thing, and what was the right? Once again I felt like a puppet whose life was being manipulated by a force I had no control over.

These stressful situations had filled my life and occupied my mind for months. And living in a small town, I continually had the feeling I was wearing that scarlet letter, that everyone knew my story and was whispering behind my back. Shopping at the supermarket, standing in line at the post office, attending events at the kids' school, I often had the sensation that people were staring at me and then quickly averting their eyes when I looked their way. It would have been so much easier, emotionally, if I had just run away from it all, moved to Nashville or some other city, and made a new life for myself. But I was determined to stay in Anderson, no matter what. I didn't want to disrupt my kids' lives any more than I already had, and there was a stubborn streak in me that made me want to stay and face whatever lay ahead so I could put it behind me and move on with my life.

There was a stubborn streak in me that made me want to stay and face whatever lay ahead so I could put it behind me and move on with my life.

Meanwhile, after I had downsized and stopped touring with backup singers, Don and his family had moved to Florida. Despite their attempts to save their own marriage, Don and his wife had also gotten divorced. He had been through the heartbreaking experience of having to tell his kids that they wouldn't be living together anymore, just as I had done. Now he was left alone and miserable in Florida but still putting on a smiley face every day as he headed off to sing happy songs at Epcot.

Sometimes, looking at all the destruction I had caused, I came close to collapsing both physically and mentally. It just all seemed too much to bear. Then I would feel myself spiritually collapsing into the arms of God, begging once again for forgiveness and grace, and every time, without fail, He set me back on my feet to take that next step toward wholeness.

As much as I was helped by my church during this time, I was also helped by the constant, enduring love of my parents. They had welcomed the kids and me into their home whenever we needed to be there and had offered a place for me to stay temporarily while I made arrangements to move out on my own. There is no way to adequately describe what their unconditional love and support have meant throughout my life. They have been my anchors in the storm, my fellow travelers on the journey, and my fellow celebrants in praising God for the joy He has brought me to today. But as close as we were, I was reluctant to tell them about my feelings for Don. Although I knew they needed to hear about it from me and not through the rumor mill, I couldn't bring myself to tell them in person. Instead I did it in a phone call. I got them both on the phone and said, "I need to tell you something. I think I'm in love with Don."

There was a long moment of silence on the other end. Then they mumbled something, and I mumbled something, and we said we loved each other and then said good-bye. That was their way. They have always been the kind of parents who love and support me no matter what I'm going through, and instead of asking a lot of in-my-face questions, they just wait until I'm ready to talk.

Having dropped the bomb by telephone, I went to their house the next day to see what kind of damage it had done. Those were the days when I seemed to be crying all the time, and while Mom was inside the house doing some laundry and puttering in the kitchen, I sat on the back porch swing, wiping away yet another round of tears.

After a while Mom quietly came out onto the porch and sat

beside me on the swing. "So, how's Don doing?" she asked without looking my way.

I smiled. "He's doing OK, I guess. He's in Florida," I said. "Thanks for asking." We continued to swing and talk for the better part of an hour. She asked how my kids were doing and how my former husband was. She also asked about Don's kids and his former wife.

In her gentle, easy way, Mom had broken the ice and let me know that she wanted to be part of my life, no matter what messes I made, no matter what difficulties I faced. Dad felt the same way. My parents certainly didn't agree with or support the choices I had made, but they let me know they were there for me, as they always have been, to see me through any situation, good or bad. Their love for me has been consistently over the top; what a wonderful blessing they have been to me and to my children.

I continued the pastoral counseling both individually and in sessions with my ex-husband and our pastors. I had benefited greatly from the help of Pastor Lyon, whose wisdom came not only from his education and his love for the Lord but also from having attended law school. From that first day when I disclosed that I had stepped across the line and had the affair, he had always talked straight with me. He didn't sugarcoat anything. And even though I didn't always like what he told me, I knew I could never find wholeness unless I was in a place where I could be confronted constantly by God's truth. So I kept showing up at those sessions, always grateful to be warmly welcomed even though I hadn't quite managed to make things right yet. Still, Pastor Lyon never said to me, "I'm not going to talk to you until you get your behavior straightened out." He kept working with me, helping me regain my footing on that rocky path toward forgiveness and healing. While he was always clear about the truth of God's Word, he was equally clear about walking with me through the process.

As I was struggling through this exhausting and stressful emotional work, and trying my best to behave as though Don were dead, as Pastor Lyon had advised, Don was going through his own healing steps. After his divorce was finalized, he and his ex-wife, Michelle, shared custody of their children. Don had moved back to Anderson, where he had been hired as fitness director at the local YMCA and where he could be closer to his kids.

Once he was back in town, it was inevitable that tentative bridges would be built and we would be drawn together again. Over the next few months we resumed our friendship and then our romance—although this time with more appropriate boundaries. As you might expect, that caused another knot in the already-tangled circumstances. Eventually it became a sweet promise, a happy portent of better times to come. But it didn't solve any of my immediate problems. The fact was, Don had asked me to marry him, and I had said yes.

We were both attending church, but separately, as we continued to confront ourselves with our past sin, to seek forgiveness and restoration, and to move back into God's loving gift of grace. Ironically, that process was about to shift into high gear, but the turning point didn't come in Pastor Lyon's office, where I sought counseling, or even in the church, where I sought sanctuary. It began that snowy night in November 1994 on the floor of the Cleveland airport.

Whatever It Takes

Surrounded by hundreds of people, I felt completely alone that night, totally empty. Something had to change. I couldn't go on with things as they were. Yet the truth seemed so hard to face . . .

I sat there on the dirty carpet, my legs drawn up and my head resting on my knees, and I cried out silently to God: *Help me, Lord. I've made such a terrible mess of things. I love You, Lord. I'm sorry, Father. Please help me. Tell me what to do.*

In my mind's eye, I can look back and see myself in that airport mob scene, and what happened next reminds me of old King Nebuchadnezzar peering into the fiery furnace and seeing the prisoners he was trying to execute, Shadrach, Meshach, and Abednego, walking around calmly amid the furious flames. The king shouted, "Look! I see *four* men walking around in the fire, unbound and unharmed, and the fourth looks like a son of the gods" (Daniel 3:25, italics added).

> *"Whatever it takes for me to be right and clean before the Lord, that's what I want to do. Whatever it takes."*

Even while I felt as though I had been engulfed by the flames of sin and ostracized by public condemnation, I suddenly sensed a peace that was beyond understanding. It was as though God were sitting there on the airport floor beside me (which, in a sense, He was), nudging me ever so gently and whispering softly to my heart, *Go ahead. I'm waiting.*

I managed to drag my stuff through the crowd then settled onto the floor beneath the bank of pay phones. I held the receiver in my hand for a moment, feeling a force of resolve build within me. I looked up Pastor Lyon's home number, punched it in, and in between every ring tone, considered ending the call. But then he answered, and my words came pouring out as though a dam had burst: "You know what? I don't care anymore," I told him. "I just don't care. I've made so many mistakes—I've divorced my husband, and I've had an affair. I've told lies, and I've hurt people. I'm tied up in knots worrying about who knows this and who knows that, and am I going to lose this and am I going to lose that? I'm sick of playing damage control, and I just can't do it anymore.

"Here's what matters to me," I continued, not even pausing to let him speak. "I want to be right and clean before the Lord. That article is going to come out; it's going to be a tell-all exposé. I've been praying that it won't be published, but now I don't care. If it is a part of the process that brings me back to a right relationship with God, then so be it. I don't care if I lose my career. I don't care if I never sing again. I don't even care if I lose Don. Whatever it takes for me to be right and clean before the Lord, that's what I want to do. Whatever it takes."

Finally I had to stop talking because the sobs had to come out. When I could speak again, I asked him, "Will you help me?"

With gentle assurance he replied, "Of course I will, Sandi."

Some people talk about the cleansing power of dropping their burdens at the foot of the cross. I know all about that marvelous, healing place; I've taken up full-time spiritual residence there. But my own journey back to Calvary came by way of the Cleveland airport. That's where I dropped my troubles at Jesus's feet: on the floor of a gate area, right beneath that bank of pay phones.

Healing Steps

I was ready to call a press conference right then and there and lay out the whole ugly mess. I was basking in the first sunbeams of freedom, and it felt so good I wanted to throw open the cell doors and go rushing out into the world shouting out every sordid detail. Thank heaven Pastor Lyon offered some wiser counsel. As we talked on the phone, and as we prayed together, I begged God to forgive me for what I had done and told the pastor I was ready to make a public confession.

"Sandi, I don't think this has to go public," he cautioned. "You've asked God to forgive you, and He has. You certainly have a responsibility to offer specific apologies to key individuals who have been harmed by your conduct. You'll need to talk to each one of them and ask their forgiveness. But I don't think you need to broadcast it; you don't need to go on CNN, because there are too many innocent bystanders, including your children, who will *not* benefit from your doing that."

To return to the Shadrach, Meshach, and Abednego analogy, I was ready to go flying out of the fiery furnace, gleefully spreading the news of my pardon to everyone who would hear it. But I was forgetting about the sparks that could fly off my smoldering rags of remorse, landing flames of pain and embarrassment on those I had already hurt by my sinful actions.

I understood the wisdom of his advice, but I still had a powerful need to confess publicly, and Pastor Lyon acknowledged that need. "As Christians we confess our sin to God, and that is enough," he said. "But there are also times when we have to acknowledge another important principle: we need to be restored to the body of Christ. Not to God—He has already forgiven us—but to His people. That is another product of confession."

He suggested a course of action that we would initiate as soon as I came home from the tour. It would begin with my appearing before the church's pastoral staff plus the twenty-four elected laypeople who comprise the church council—a total of about thirty-five people. Then, in the presence of others (often the "witnesses" were Pastor Lyon and the other person's pastor), I would apologize to and ask forgiveness of specific people who had been hurt by my actions. Two of those people were my ex-husband and Don's former wife. After that I would meet regularly with an accountability group of church people and friends who would hold me to the course of action I had committed to.

Pastor Lyon ended the call by assuring me he would stick with me and help me through the restoration process. "I'm not going anywhere," he said. "I'll be here for you." And then he repeated the words I had already heard from him again and again: "Be encouraged, Sandi."

I felt unimaginable relief, knowing I had taken the first real step toward wholeness. John 8:32 says, "The truth will set you free," and I immediately felt the reality of those words. I was indeed encouraged, and I was getting that first wonderful taste of freedom from the anxiety I'd been carrying around for all those months.

When I returned to the tour the next day, even though I hadn't made it home to see my children, I felt like a completely different person. Well-known pastor and best-selling author Max Lucado was traveling with the Young Messiah Tour that year; as far as I know it was his one and only time to be a part of it. To me it seemed God had put him there at the specific time I needed him.

One day I asked him if we might get together to talk about a situation I was involved in. "I'd just like to share with you some things that are going on in my life," I told him.

By the way he responded to my request, Max taught me an important lesson and also encouraged me tremendously as he was doing it. What he did probably seems perfectly logical to all of you who have been blessed with a normal amount of common sense, but obviously I have already shown that certain types of wisdom just weren't in abundance in my head at that point. Without saying so, I assumed we would meet either in Max's hotel room or mine. Of course that wasn't proper; not at all. But that fact just never occurred to me.

I can hold on and be blown off, or I can let go and see what happens.

Max said, "I'll meet you downstairs, and we can go to a little coffee shop around the corner." He was setting our meeting in a very public place where we could also have privacy. That was the important lesson, and today I make sure I abide by it. In my career there are many times when I need to meet with male business contacts or assistants, but I am careful to avoid situations where I'm alone with any man except my husband so there is never any question of decency and propriety.

That day I laid out my situation to Max, including the fact that sooner or later an article was going to be published. "I don't want to back away from anything, Max," I told him. "I know I'm heading into some severe consequences. But I want to go into them with all the wisdom I can gather for how I need to deal with this."

"Sandi, I know you understand sin, and I know you understand the consequences," he said. "It sounds like you've finally made some good decisions about the path you need to follow. But that's not what we're talking about here. Anybody who's going to read this article is not going to be able to be part of your healing process. So it's going to do them no good to have this published."

And it obviously wasn't going to do *me* any good either. Max's understanding words were an awesome gift to me. They reenforced the comments Pastor Lyon had made, and once again I came away feeling warmly encouraged that my feelings had been understood.

Making Choices

It was around that time that I had the first of two amazing dreams. I found myself in a bleak, barren desert, standing on the edge of a precipice. Below me the earth dropped away into a chasm that went forever and ever. As I teetered on the edge of the cliff, I grabbed onto a craggy old tree, a plant that showed no signs of life whatsoever.

Then a storm came up. The wind was fierce, and it blew the tree over so it was only attached to the cliff by the thinnest tendril of root. I was terrified, but at the same time I was thinking, *All right. I can hold on and be blown off, or I can let go and see what happens.* It wasn't a good set of options, but in my dream I was grateful just to have a choice.

I decided to let go, and the wind swirled mightily around me as I fell. In just a second or two, I felt my feet touch the ground. I looked around and was amazed. The wind had changed so that

I no longer hung over the precipice but stood on solid ground. I had landed safely.

It could have been something spicy I'd eaten for dinner that night. But I preferred to think of the dream as a heavenly gift of love and encouragement, illustrating how God sometimes changes the direction of the "wind" in our lives and brings us out of harm and into safety. Most importantly, the dream helped me see that I had choices. I remembered thinking in the dream, *I'll fall if I have to, but at least it's MY CHOICE whether to hang on or let go!*

When the Young Messiah Tour was over, I found myself again in Pastor Lyon's office, ready to begin the steps he had outlined for public confession and restoration to the church. I had said that I would give up my relationship with Don if that's what it took to stand clean before the Lord. Pastor Lyon didn't say I had to do that, but he helped me consider all sides of the situation.

When he had proposed, Don had dropped onto one knee and offered me a beautiful diamond ring. But recognizing all the challenges we faced—and all the emotional baggage I was still dragging around—I did something I didn't really want to do but knew was the best thing for both of us.

I returned the ring.

When my plans have fallen through
and when my strength is nearly gone,
When there's nothing left to do
but just depend on you, and the power of your name,
There is strength in the name of the Lord.
There is power in the name of the Lord.
There is hope in the name of the Lord.
—Phil McHugh, Gloria Gaither, Sandi Patty Helvering
"In the Name of the Lord"

Chapter Seven

RESETTING THE CLOCK

Even though I had returned the engagement ring, Don and I talked by phone a few times as Christmas approached. Our conversations were strained. He was taking his kids to West Virginia to visit relatives there; my kids would be with their dad. So I would be spending Christmas Eve alone.

I went to church that night, then came home and sat alone in the living room with no lights on except the strings of colorful bulbs on the Christmas tree. You might guess that I felt sad, but I didn't. It was a precious time of thoughtful reflection and prayer as I considered all the tremendous gifts I had been given: four wonderful children, a rewarding career, and most valuable of all—I picked up the little baby Jesus out of the nativity set—forgiveness and hope. "On this night You were born for *me*," I whispered, gratitude filling my heart.

Later that week I had the second amazing dream. I was there in the living room again, sitting alone beside the tree, but something was different. In the corner of the room was an old, dead, pitiful-looking plant in a pot, something so ugly it should have been thrown away. There was no life in it at all.

Under the Christmas tree, there was a single package wrapped in tin foil, with a little bow. I knew the package was for me; it was a gift to me from the baby Jesus. But when I opened the box, it was full of manure! I was shocked. *Thanks a lot, Lord. Why are You giving me this? Don't I have enough of it in my life already?*

In my dream Jesus took the package from me, walked over to the ugly plant, and spread the manure over the soil in the pot. Suddenly that plant grew and grew and grew until it became a tree that was touching the ceiling. Then Jesus took the foil wrapping and fashioned it into a star that He placed on top of the tree. Seeing it there I knew that, although there was still a lot of manure to be dealt with in my life, everything was going to be OK. The greenest grass and the most beautiful trees have been surrounded by manure during their growth process.

Apologies and Resolution

The church council was holding its regular meeting at Pastor Lyon's house in late December 1994, and my name was at the top of the agenda. Although my appearance before the council was bound by strict confidentiality, I had welcomed the support of the leaders of my parish group when they offered it. To help members of the congregation get acquainted, the church's membership is organized into groups of neighbors who live in the same general area. Although when my parish-group friends offered their help, they didn't know what my visit before the council was about—and they didn't ask questions—they still offered to pick me up and drive me to the council meeting. They also offered to wait outside until the meeting was over, but I invited them in, grateful for their loving gesture of support.

As the meeting started, Pastor Lyon described the process I had begun. He didn't believe a public confession to the whole church body was necessary, he said, because the council members had been elected by the church body to represent all the members of the church. These church representatives weren't related to me through either family or business, so they had nothing to gain or lose by speaking the truth to me. The pastor added that an article was probably going to appear in the national media, and he said he didn't want it to catch the church family off guard.

Then he invited me to speak. The council members let me tell my story without interruption. I was so embarrassed to have to tell them what I had done. The shame I felt that night was something dark and ugly and despicable. I told the council members that Don and I had had an "inappropriate relationship" while I had been married to my husband and that I had lied to hide that fact.

The only sound in the room was my faltering voice, occasionally punctuated by pauses and sobs as I awkwardly explained the horrible mess that had consumed me for more than two years.

Then there were a few questions. They wanted to know if my confession was sincere and where I was now on my journey toward healing and in my relationship with Don.

I described the accountability group I had set up to help me continue my journey toward restoration: I had suggested some names, and Pastor Lyon had suggested some others, and from that list we had agreed upon five church members who would meet with me regularly to verify my efforts and validate my progress.

The council members were supportive of the plan. They helped me identify key individuals and business contacts I needed to meet with and apologize to. Then they encouraged me, prayed for me, and sent me on my way riding yet another tremendous wave of relief.

After the holidays I began making appointments with those key people. One of them was my ex-husband, to whom I apologized in front of our pastors. Another apology went to Don's ex-wife, Michelle. It began with a letter from me and later included a face-to-face conversation. Our meeting was not an easy one, but Michelle responded with forgiveness and grace, and that attitude has continued in the years since then. She and Don have taken care to show each other respect and consideration so their children know with certainty that their well-being is always foremost in their parents' minds.

I made an apology call to the executives at my record label. Not only did I have to confess that I had been involved in an affair, I also had to acknowledge that I had lied to them when they asked about the rumors. And that wasn't all: they needed to know about the impending article because it certainly had the potential to impact my product sales.

I wouldn't have been surprised if they had responded with indignant anger and curtly warned me that I would be hearing from their lawyers. Instead, they assured me of their prayers and suggested simply that we take a break and delay the release of my next album. "Let's let it [the article] hit the fan and see what happens," one of them told me. Their position of support during this time was largely due to the steps I had already taken with my pastor and my church family.

In addition to making the apologies, I also started meeting with my accountability group. At the meetings, my accountability partners would ask what struggles I had faced the previous week. The procedure was also that each week I would give them three questions to ask me at our next meeting: straightforward, yes-or-no queries that targeted specific problem areas. I would pick those questions and say, "These are the areas in which I need you to hold me accountable." Then the session would end with their asking, "How can we pray for you this coming week?"

You might be interested to know that I continued to meet with that accountability group until November 1997.

Life in the Psych Ward: "What Do You Need?"

Although I had broken my engagement to Don, my feelings for him hadn't changed. But if we were to have a future together—that is, if he was still interested—I knew I didn't want to start a second marriage with the same old emotional garbage I had hauled into my first one, plus all the stuff ensuing from that troubled relationship and the resulting divorce. To get rid of it, I would need professional help.

I made arrangements with my ex-husband for our children to stay with him while I received therapy at a Minirth-Meier Clinic in St. Louis for two weeks. I have to admit: I arrived there with an attitude. Sitting on the floor of my room with a chaplain the first day, I poured out the troubling events of my past—the episode of childhood abuse, the difficulties in my marriage, and the poor choices that had led to the affair—and complained, "Where was God in all of this?"

The chaplain was good. He let me rant and rave and go on and on, railing against God. Occasionally, when I paused for a breath, he would say things like, "It ain't any big deal. God can handle it. Tell Him! Tell Him you're ticked off at Him. Go ahead. You won't be the first one, and you won't be the last. Go for it." It felt much like children would feel when they're angry at a parent for setting down a few rules. Children can only rant and rave if, deep down, they know the parent loves them unconditionally.

> *During the next couple of weeks, I was able to work through my feelings from beginning to end.*

When I'd finally let it all out, he gave me an amazing book, Philip Yancey's *Disappointment with God.* What validation I felt, knowing I had been heard and understood. During the next couple of weeks, I was able to work through my feelings from beginning to end, uninterrupted by the timer going off on the stove or the phone ringing or someone needing to be delivered to dance practice or choir rehearsal.

I not only benefited, myself, from my experience at the clinic, but I also learned some things that guided me afterward in reaching out to friends and family members who were encountering similar difficulties. For example, at Minirth-Meier, whenever anybody would be in a very emotional state, the therapist would ask, "What do you need right now?"

I've tried to do that with my friends, asking them when they are going through a tough time, "What do you need?"

Of course the answer isn't always easy to come by. I remember telling one counselor at the clinic, "I don't know what I need. I need to keep talking a little more."

"OK," she said. "Keep talking."

Another time I snapped, "I need to get out of this place!"

"OK, go ahead. The doors aren't locked."

The staff quickly realized how important being able to make my own choices was to me. So that was part of my program, being placed in situations that encouraged me to exert my choice and then having that option validated. The result was a conversation with a therapist that went something like this:

"I don't even know why I'm here."

"OK. What do you need?"

"I don't want to be here."

"OK. What do you need to make that happen?"

"I need to be able to walk out the door."

"Well, go ahead."

I walked out the door, down the stairs, and marched out of the building. The therapist followed me.

I stood there awhile, silently fuming. Eventually she asked again, "What do you need?"

"I need to go back inside and work," I moaned.

"OK then," she answered. "Let's go do it."

It sounds a lot like this mother of four was acting like a child in the throes of the terrible twos, doesn't it? But through these seemingly childish episodes, I was processing the obstacles that had held me back ever since, as a little girl, I had begun believing that I had no choice but to submit when others placed their desires over mine. It seemed quite difficult at the time, but as I look back, I see the tremendous strides I made toward emotional recovery during those days. I think of it as the best work I've ever done. There, among the other "walking wounded" and the caring professionals who devoted their careers to helping us, I found extraordinary grace and acceptance—even more than I'd felt in many churches. At the clinic, those of us who sought treatment were free to be wherever we were in our journey, and because our sense of acceptance was so great, when the therapists gently nudged us to take the next step, or even when there was confrontation, we were able to receive it for what it was: not as criticism but as help.

In the psych ward, I learned how to reset the imaginary clock that had become the basis of many of my emotional responses as an adult.

I'm not offering this explanation as an excuse for the poor choices I did make when I finally claimed the right to think for myself. Making excuses means I'm still being controlled and victimized by what happened, and I've moved beyond that barrier. With the help of talented, dedicated therapists; my amazing parents; an insightful, godly pastor; and a church congregation that has loved, supported, and guided me through years of apology, forgiveness, and restoration, I have come to embrace the freedom that comes with God's unconditional love and unfathomable grace, even as an ugly truth is brought out into the open.

There was another difficult thing I needed to do to make a fresh start. I had to tell my parents about the abuse I had endured at the hands of the baby-sitter. It had occurred more than thirty years earlier, but I knew it would still be tragic news for them. I could only imagine how devastated I would be to have my children tell me something like that, and I knew they would think, *It's our fault. We should have seen it. How could we have misjudged this person so completely and entrusted our daughter to her care?*

As expected, they were greatly grieved by the shocking news when I finally told them. But they understood that if I was going to get rid of all the ugly baggage in my past, they had to be included in my healing process. They gladly agreed to come to the counselor with me a few times, not only to show their support, but so she could say to them, "There's no way you could have seen that coming. It was *not* your fault." My parents have been and continue to be the most loving, caring, supportive, and resilient people I've ever known.

Starting Over

I came home from Minirth-Meier refreshed and strong, ready to move confidently into the next chapter of my life, whatever it held. I fulfilled the few concert bookings that were scheduled, resumed the meetings with my accountability group, prayed constantly to God to praise Him for His mercy and thank Him for His forgiveness, and continued to seek guidance and encouragement from Pastor Lyon.

How wonderful it was to feel happy and in control. In this confident, positive state of mind, it seemed only natural to want to share my newfound attitude by letting Don know the good things that were going on in my life. I was so very glad to see him again.

During the next couple of months, we talked frequently and went out several times. It felt good to be together again, although things weren't always rosy; we still had several issues to work through. But I was encouraged to see that we could resolve our conflicts without tempers flaring or angry words being thrown about, as had occurred during conflicts in my first marriage. For the first time in more than a decade, I was enjoying a nurturing, devoted relationship similar to the one I had seen Mom and Dad model throughout my life.

Increasingly, when we were together, all seven of our kids were with us too. They had known each other most of their lives, either because Don and I sometimes brought our families along when we worked together or because the kids had gotten acquainted in school or at things like gym-and-swim at the YMCA. Don had created a Friday-night event for his kids that they called "Super Wind-Down," and my four kids and I eagerly joined in. It was a weekly pizza, popcorn, rented-movie, slumber-party evening with everyone sacked out in sleeping bags on the living-room floor.

At one of these gatherings, Anna must have sensed that things were coming together again for us. As we all sprawled around the room munching popcorn, she suddenly blurted out, "OK, so are you guys gonna get married or not?"

There was an instant hush as seven pairs of eyes turned toward Don and me. I smiled at him and shrugged. He smiled at me and shrugged back. We turned to look at the youngsters, sitting as still as statues, waiting for the answer.

"Well . . . yeah, I guess we are," he said.

I nodded.

The kids let out a cheer and then, as Don pulled me into his arms for a kiss, they all, being kids, ran around the room shrieking, "Eeeeeuuuuuuuuuuuu! Gross!"

Top left: Sandi as a baby, 1958. *Top right:* Sandi, two years old.
Bottom: (left to right) Sandi, Mike, and Craig Patty, 1961.

THE RON PATTY FAMILY

Top: The Patty kids in concert in the late 1960s. (Note the white go-go boots.)
Bottom: *The Ron Patty Family* album cover, 1972.

Top Left: Sandi in high school, 1974. *Top Right:* The Patty kids on the road, 1973. *Bottom: The Ron Patty Family* album cover, 1973.

Top: Sandi with her parents the evening she wins her first Grammy Award in 198

Bottom Left: Sandi in 1982 with her first Dove Award,
which honored her as Female Vocalist of the Year.

Bottom Right: Sandi won three Dove Awards in 1987: Gospel Artist of the Year
Female Vocalist of the Year, and Inspirational Album of the Year for *Morning Like*

Left: Sandi, pregnant with Anna at the 1984 Dove Awards program, celebrates with Lanny Wolfe, who won Song of the Year honors for composing "More Than Wonderful," which Sandi recorded with Larnelle Harris. Sandi won for Female Vocalist of the Year.

Bottom Left: Sandi during a telephone interview, 1986.
Bottom Right: Sandi's mother makes a surprise visit to a Maine performace, 1989.

Top: Sandi in the kitchen with her four children, 1991.
Bottom: Sandi with her mother on Sandi's thirtieth birthday.

Top: Sandi with then–Vice President Bush, 1986.
Bottom: Sandi's first visit with Johnny Carson on the *Tonight Show,* 1986.

Top: The Patty kids, all grown up, at Craig's wedding, 1994.
Bottom: In 1996 Sandi and her brothers surprised their parents to celebrate Ron and Carolyn Patty's birthdays, which are one day apart.

Top Left and Right: Sandi and Don on a Bermuda cruise, 1997.
Bottom: Ron and Carolyn Patty with Sandi and Don, Bermuda, 1997.

Above: Family vacation to Yellowstone National Park, 1997.

Top: Sandi and Don with the Clintons at the second inauguration, 1997.
Sandi sang the national anthem at the inaugural gala.
Bottom: The Patty family in Phoenix, Arizona, 1998.

Top: Sandi and Don at the first Bush inauguration, 2001.
Sandi sang the national anthem at the beginning of the inaugural festivities.
Bottom: Family vacation in Estes Park, Colorado, 1997.

Left: In 2004 Sandi began singing—and signing— an updated version of "We Shall Behold Him."

Middle: The Gospel Music Association Hall of Fame medallions (front, *left;* back, *right*) presented in 2004.
Bottom: In 2004 Sandi was inducted into the Gospel Music Hall of Fame by Dottie Rambo, composer of "We Shall Behold Him."

Top: Family vacation, Epcot Center, 2001.
Bottom: Family vacation, Jamaica, 2003.

Family vacation, the Grand Canyon, 2004.

Anna and Jennifer

Jonathan

Sandi and Don

Donnie

Aly

Erin

Sam

Mollie

Let this be our prayer, when we lose our way:
Lead us to the place, guide us with your grace
To a place where we'll be safe.
I pray we'll find your light and hold it in our hearts
When stars go out each night, remind us where you are.
—Carole Bayer Sager and David Foster
"The Prayer"

Chapter Eight

UGLY TRUTH, BEAUTIFUL FREEDOM

The wedding, held outdoors on August 6, 1995, in beautiful Estes Park, Colorado, was two hours long. In addition to the traditional wedding vows, Don and I had written vows that we read to each other and vows that we read to our own kids and vows that we read to our new stepkids. Then the kids read sweet little vows to us. There were vows flying all over the place! Right up there with the birth and (later) the adoption days of my children, it was one of the best, most deliriously happy days of my life.

We were surrounded by a joyful army of family and friends who gathered with us in a beautiful courtyard outside a huge, rustic lodge where we were staying; the backdrop was a spectacular view of the mountains painted by God Himself. Many of our wedding guests were staying with us in the lodge (it sleeps twenty-five people). Others were staying in cabins down the road.

Don and I would slip away for one night alone then rejoin the rest of the group, with everyone invited to stay over for a few days and share what we were calling our "familymoon." (With seven kids, we figured there was no use trying to have a lot of privacy, so why not just invite the whole army to join us for the post-wedding celebration?)

My three close-as-sisters girlfriends, Shari Schrock, Carolyn Gill, and Laura Hammel-Riggs—I call them my "ya-yas"—were there with their entire families, along with both my brothers and their families, and of course, my parents. Our beloved nanny, Betty Fair, joined us, and best of all, her husband, Phil, an ordained pastor, officiated at the ceremony and pronounced us husband and wife.

My family filled most of the seats. But some special friends were there for Don. He was an adopted only child, and both of his parents had passed away years earlier, so he had no one from his family to be there for him. But a wonderful Greek couple whom he had met through his work at the Y asked if they could attend the wedding and stand in for his Greek adoptive parents (who would be watching from heaven), and Don gratefully accepted.

The precious stand-in parents made sure we included all the best components of a traditional Greek wedding. Don escorted them in and seated them on the front row, where his parents would have sat if they had been there. The couple even gave Don a Greek coin to give to me because on the wedding day, the groom's parents traditionally give a gift to the bride. I later had that coin made into a necklace. What a poignantly beautiful part of that day they were.

When the ceremony concluded and the partying wound down,

Don and I made our exit. But when we returned the next day, we were met with sad faces and unimaginably sad news.

One of our wedding guests was Janice Sutton, our devoted housekeeper. While Betty had kept the kids, Janice had kept our house, coming regularly to keep it clean and orderly—or at least as clean and orderly as a house with four kids could be. After the divorce, she had continued to work for both my ex-husband and me; she was such a dynamo, she could clean two houses in the time others struggled to finish one.

When we returned the next day, we were met with sad faces and unimaginably sad news.

Janice had rarely traveled outside Indiana, and she was delighted to be included in the wedding party. She laughed and danced and bubbled over with appreciation for the spectacular scenery at Estes Park and for the wonderful warmth of friendship we all shared during the wedding celebration.

When Don and I rejoined the group that morning after the wedding, we knew immediately that something was wrong. "What is it?" I asked quickly as I braced myself for bad news.

"It's Janice," Phil told me gently. He and the others had been concerned when she hadn't appeared for breakfast or throughout the rest of the morning. Finally he and Betty had gone into her room and found her lifeless, fully clothed body lying on the floor. Phil immediately started CPR as Betty ran for Shari, a nurse-practitioner. Although she and Phil worked frantically to revive her, Janice was gone. Doctors told us later that she had died instantly of an aneurysm.

It was a shocking, difficult loss, and as we flew back to Indiana a few days later, our happiness to be starting a new life together was tinged with the sorrow of losing a friend.

As we arrived back in Anderson, I felt content and confident, looking forward to the next chapter of my life with Don. We were ready to build a new life and a new home together, hoping the difficult days were behind us and a new life of happiness and wholeness lay ahead. But when we got home, I learned what the reporter had been waiting for before releasing the article: a wedding. Apparently the exposé would be published in *Christianity Today* sometime in the next few weeks.

The Day We Were the Sermon

When I had first learned about the impending article several months earlier, I figured I had nothing to lose by calling the reporter. "Please don't do this," I said. "I don't care so much about me. I deserve whatever happens to me. But you're going to hurt some other people, and that's not right."

He replied, "I need to tell the whole story. Just by your calling and saying that, you've pretty much confirmed that it's all true."

I had urged him to call Pastor Lyon and verify the steps I had taken to seek forgiveness, healing, and restoration to the church. The reporter had done that and had also exchanged letters with Pastor Lyon, who had urged him not to publish the article. In a four-page letter dated August 3, 1995 (three days before Don and I were married), Pastor Lyon cited "the parameters of biblical principles, outlined in Matthew 18" and stated, "Your informants and sources should confront Sandi directly with their concerns before publishing their charges." He also pointed out that I had agreed to face my accusers but that none had been willing to confront me directly. Until that happened, Pastor Lyon said, "publishing their concerns and judgments might fairly be described as gossip."

He also wrote, "She has assumed responsibility for her failures—for her sin, without excuse. She has humiliated herself with astonishing transparency before a most intimidating audience: her local church council. . . . Few are they in this world—or in the Kingdom—who would voluntarily make themselves available for such examination."

But nothing would dissuade the reporter from submitting the article for publication. Don and I talked it over with Pastor Lyon and decided that if the truth was going to come out, we would stand to face the consequences. We agreed that he would address our church about the issue on Sunday. Meanwhile the impending article was outlined to the national media, and on Saturday morning the local newspaper carried this front-page headline: "Gospel singer Sandi Patty goes public, admits affair."

That evening before Don and I were to face the church and own the truth about what we had done, Pastor Lyon came to our house to talk about what would happen Sunday morning. We sat around a table. Don was strong and stoic, but I was terrified at the prospect of how the congregation might react to the ugly story it was about to hear. "I don't know if I can do this," I said, feeling broken and afraid.

"Yes, you can," Pastor Lyon assured me. "The truth always heals, even if it's hard to bear. The Lord will stand with you, Sandi, as you bow before Him. He will honor you for being true."

The pastor gently reviewed with us how his sermon would play out. He said he had tried to find a story less obvious than John's Gospel account of the woman caught in adultery, but in the end her story had so many parallels to mine that it was the only choice. He was thinking of how Jesus had stood by that woman and how He would stand by me too.

At the end of the evening, I was trembling with anxiety but again full of resolve. I rested my arms on the table and dropped my head onto them: "I'll do it," I moaned. "I have to do it. But I'm so afraid."

Before Pastor Lyon left, he prayed a simple prayer that the Lord would be glorified, that the devil's power would be broken, and that healing would come. We were living out the stark reality of sin's cost—and the hope Jesus brings.

The bucket was full of big, smooth river rocks.

Later that night I called my friend Shari and ruefully quipped, "Just what does one wear to a stoning? I could wear white, but that seems a little presumptuous. I could wear red, but that's a little obvious." (You have to have a sense of humor through the minefields of life, or you'll surely go mad.)

I settled on green. I suppose that symbolized new life to me.

The next morning was September 3, 1995, almost a month to the day after our beautiful Colorado wedding. Riding to church, I mused over the range of emotions I'd felt in those four short weeks, from a joy-filled Rocky Mountain high to the sorrow over Janice's death to my current state of nervousness. Don was trying hard to be strong for both of us, but I could tell he was nervous too. How thankful I was that he was as determined as I was to take these steps toward restoration, no matter what difficulties the truth unleashed upon us.

We got to church early, settled the kids in their Sunday school classes, and quietly took our seats on the front pew. (How I wished we could be on the back row of the balcony that morning!) By the time the pastor stepped forward to begin the sermon, my palms were sweaty and my heart was pounding. He smiled our way and gave us an encouraging nod. Then, from behind the pulpit, he brought out a heavy metal bucket and set it on the communion table. Although the rest of the congregation probably couldn't see inside, I knew what it contained.

The bucket was full of big, smooth river rocks.

Pastor Lyon has given me permission to quote from his sermon here. I wish there were space to include every word of it; instead I can share only a brief, edited excerpt.[1] If you're not in the mood for an amazing lesson about sin, confession, and grace, just skip to the end of this chapter. But as for me, his words, now almost ten years later, still carry the same strong, healing message that touched my heart when I first heard them in person, sitting on the front row of the church. He said:

This morning, with Sandi's permission, I'd like to use her story as an illustration of a text. I wrestled long and hard, after her story was to be made public, about how to approach the church with it because, well, it just needs to be told here, now that you're going to read about it in the paper. And the story you read yesterday in the *Herald Bulletin* [the local newspaper] is just the tip of the iceberg in terms of media accounts and stories and tales people will tell.

You'll be besieged, I suppose, in the next few weeks, maybe even months, with all kinds of things other people have said. Well, I want you to hear it as I understand it. And so today Sandi is here with Don Peslis, her husband, on the front row, and I'm going to use them as an illustration of a scripture, John 8:1–11:

"Jesus went to the Mount of Olives. At dawn he appeared again in the temple courts, where all the people gathered around him, and he sat down to teach them. The teachers of the law and the Pharisees brought in a woman caught in adultery. They made her stand before the group and said to Jesus, 'Teacher, this woman was caught in the act of adultery. In the Law Moses commanded us to stone such women. Now what do you say?' They were using this question as a trap in order to have a basis for accusing him.

"But Jesus bent down and started to write on the ground with his finger. When they kept on questioning him, he straightened up and said to them, 'If any one of you is without sin, let him be the first to throw a stone at her.' Again he stooped down and wrote on the ground.

"At this, those who heard began to go away one at a time, the older ones first, until only Jesus was left, with the woman still standing there. Jesus straightened up and asked her, 'Woman, where are they? Has no one condemned you?'

"'No one, sir,' she said.

"'Then neither do I condemn you,' Jesus declared. 'Go now and leave your life of sin.'"

The story gives us some very important truths. The first thing about it is that sin happens, and it happens sometimes in our own midst. Wherever you have a group of people, you're going to have sin.

My job is to help people who fall into sin find their way out again. That's a little different definition of the job than perhaps some of you have. That's how I've interpreted my role. This church has sin in it. There is sin that was present before I came. There is new sin that's happened since I got here. There'll be new sin that I can't even foresee. There's sin in the body of Christ, and let's admit it. The facts are, sin happens, and Jesus was in a world where the people of God were rife with sin.

Another thing this story demonstrates is that sin is of great curiosity. People have a kind of prurient interest in other people's sins. . . . Some people aren't content just to be fascinated by others' sin. They have to make sure everybody is fascinated by it. They have to be sure everybody knows the whole story. That really is bothersome to me. It's one thing to be fascinated in silence by another person's sin. It's quite another to feel it needs to be propelled into the public eye. . . .

There are some journalists who have even, in my view, held it over Sandi almost like blackmail, saying, in essence, "If you don't do what we want, then we're going to do this."

I find that outrageous. My position has been, to all the journalists with whom I've spoken, "How do you know about these things? Who told you this stuff?"

"Well, we can't reveal our sources. They're unnamed. They're anonymous."

Well, I think, according to Scripture, if a person has a

problem with someone, he needs to speak to that person directly. I will guarantee you that Sandi Patty will speak to anyone who has a problem with choices she has made. If people are aware of sin in her life, let them step forward, and she'll speak to them.

"Well, we've tried that before," the journalists would say. "Our sources say they tried before, but she would not hear them."

It's true. There was a time in Sandi's life when she was in denial. She covered up her original sin of adultery with a second sin of deceit. And that was very wrong also. So I understand how those people might feel. But then I said, a year and a half ago, "Well, I'll guarantee you that she'll face it now. And if she will not face it, then I will change my position. But until those people step forward and give her a chance to meet them face to face, I myself will oppose publication of this story."

I took that to our church council also, and they voted unanimously last December to oppose any publication of her story, thinking it was not right—unless people first stepped forward and identified themselves. And I want you to know, since June of 1994, only one person stepped forward out of the shadows to say, "You know what, Sandi? I have some trouble with what you've done."

I sat in a meeting where she confessed her sin to him, and they talked and we prayed, and then that person said, "I'm satisfied. I don't need to say anything more about this at all."

And that, my friends, is appropriate restitution.

But except for that one, no other person in this town, no other member of any family anywhere, as far as I know, has come to her and said, "This is my problem with you."

I want you to know that Sandi Patty, whatever she has done, is standing up and saying, "I did it. And there are no excuses. And I am ashamed."

And for all of those who fed the media, wherever you are, whoever you are out there, I challenge you and dare you to stand up also and own responsibility for speaking about people in complete violation of the Scripture. Sandi has violated the Scripture. There's no doubt

Sandi Patty is standing up and saying, "I did it. And there are no excuses. And I am ashamed."

about that. But this church is not, with a wink and a nod, indulging gross sin. Absolutely not. When it was drawn to my attention that she had done these things and she owned responsibility for it, this church lifted up the Scripture to her face, and she read it and understood it.

And when she has, in the process of healing and restoration, not always been what I wished she'd be, it wasn't because I just bowed my head and said, "Sandi, oh, no problem." She knows. I spoke to her the truth of my heart. The Scriptures here have been elevated. The Word has been made true. We need to all obey the whole of Scripture, not just parts.

This Scripture passage tells us about how some people

just have to make sure that others know; so as it became clear that Sandi's story was going to be told anyway, she has cooperated with the media and stepped forward to own, in a public way, her sin. And that's why it was in the newspaper yesterday. That's why it's on the AP wire. That's why you'll hear more about it. It's a terrible tale, an awful story.

Imagine yourself in some gross violation of God's law that is completely incongruent with what you have represented over a lifetime. Imagine yourself going and standing before a group of persons, church officers, and owning responsibility and telling them what you've done.

Sandi has exposed herself in that way. And it's been horrifying.

Some people feel that, in the face of sin, it is the responsibility of the body of Christ to exact retribution, to punish, that there must be some kind of punitive sentence when people sin: You know, he or she needs to pay. That one who wronged me needs to pay. All of this is a kind of exacting of judgment on people.

But this story teaches us that Jesus was not interested in involving the body of Christ in punitive measures for people who admit their sin. Now, follow what I say carefully: There are times in the Scripture where the church is required to discipline its members who *hide* in sin. But for those who admit their wrongdoing, for those who own responsibility for their sin, well, then, Jesus had a few words. . . .

He stood up and said—I'm paraphrasing here—"Well, if you must have a reply, how about this one? You who have no sin, why don't you be the first one to pick up a stone?"

He was saying, in effect, "If there's but one among you who's righteous, come on down. Come forward. Here they are. Is there someone in this room who would like to come and get the stone from me? Just take it out of my hand. We don't all have to be righteous. Just one of you. Just one."

I must confess before you: I am not worthy. I stand before you by the grace of God and the cleansing blood of Jesus Christ. I stand by the cross. I'm not worthy to pick up a stone. But maybe one of you is better than I am.

"Is there someone in this room who would like to come and get the stone from me? Just take it out of my hand."

Is there judgment in your heart? Is there a price that needs to be paid? Is there something that must be done? The rocks are there. I think it would be important, before you leave here today and begin processing and complaining and judging and criticizing and making all kinds of tales, to think about this story. Think about the story of Jesus Christ and this woman. Think about Sandi Patty. Think about the shame she has brought on herself, her children, her family, her church, her record company, her Lord.

And Don Peslis in the same way. Oh, he's not been on a world stage in the same way, but he has shamed his family also. And his Lord, his church, and all those who have ever trusted him.

Think about that. It's awful. Awful. Makes my heart

break. Think about your shame. And then think about Jesus Christ, who is the exact representation of God Himself. Think about how He faced an adulteress who brought shame on her family. "Where are your accusers?" He asked. "Has no one risen up to pick up a stone?"

"No one, sir," she said very deferentially. This was a woman who bore witness by her speech of the contriteness of her heart, the humility of her soul.

"Then neither do I condemn you," said Jesus. "Go. And don't ever do this again."

And so does the Lord say to all of us, "Neither do I condemn you. Go, and sin no more."

This morning as we bring this service to a close, think about this church, how we should be. Think about how we should respond in the face of sin that—well, it happens. What can we do to make sure it happens with less frequency over time?

I'm going to sit on the step here, and I want you to imagine Christ sitting here right now—He is. And Sandi's here; she's on the front row. She's been exposed. She's been humiliated. The truth has been told. This is where we are. Is there anything more you think she should do? What can she do to make it right? If you don't feel satisfied that this is a chapter now closed, you need to walk up at the end and get a stone. I don't expect you to throw it at her. But you need to own your own feelings, and you need to take that stone and give it to her. And by so doing, you're going to say, "I'm not right with this yet."

In the story of David and Bathsheba, the prophet of God confronts the wayward king and says, in effect, "You know, David, you blew it big time."

David prayed to die because his heart was so appalled at the choices he had made. David and Bathsheba went on, but the scars of their sin haunted them for as long as they lived. Nobody had to intervene and say, "You need to suffer more."

Sin always carries with it a terrible price. But it is the glory of God that He heals and forgives. I guess maybe that's what He'd like His body to do also.

Benediction

The church service was nearly over. But before Pastor Lyon dismissed the congregation, he prayed, "Our Father, we thank You for the priceless gift of Your love. We are frail and flawed and unable to see as clearly as You do. As a pastor, Lord, I don't always do my job just right. I'm not always everything I need to be as a pastor. I'm not always the husband, the father, the person You need me to be. But Lord, You know I want to be! And I suppose everyone in this room could pray that way. Help us, Lord. We pray that our church may be what You want it to be, no matter what the world outside thinks we should be. We pray in Jesus's name. Amen."

The church members silently filed out of the building—except for one man, who came to the front, lifted a rock out of the bucket, and handed it to me.

Who can rescue me from all that I've become?
Thanks to Heaven it's already done.
—Bob Farrell and Greg Nelson
"The Dilemma"

Chapter Nine

FACING THE MUSIC

Our church holds two services on Sunday, so we were the sermon topic not once but twice that long Sunday morning. After the first service, the man who had handed me the stone emerged from the building and stood in the parking lot, wondering why no one else had followed suit. He had misunderstood the instructions and thought that handing me a stone indicated that he had no problem with the steps toward restoration that I had taken. He thought by handing it back he was signaling that he wouldn't be throwing stones at me! The poor guy was so embarrassed when he discovered what he'd done that he hurried back inside to make amends. It was exactly what we needed at that moment—a gift of laughter to fortify us for the second round of facing the music.

We stepped out into the sunshine that day feeling forgiven, loved, and challenged to take the next step. As Pastor Lyon said to me later, "If the church is to be a judging place, then it's about 'Well, that happened.' But if you get focused on that, you can never be redeemed. Instead it seems to me that Jesus is always about 'Well, now what?' He says, in essence, 'Here you are, woman condemned of adultery. Now what? Go and sin no more.' I guess that's all of our stories."

> *My record label decided to postpone the release of my upcoming Christmas album.*

He said he would like our church to be known as the "And-Now-What? Church."

Christianity Today published the tell-all article in its next issue, dated September 11, 1995.

The firestorm began; the story was picked up by the national press and appeared in newspapers everywhere. Concert bookings were being canceled left and right. The radio stations that had still been airing my music after the divorce now pulled it off their play lists. I was told that some churches sent out letters to their mailing lists, informing their members of what I had done and urging them not to attend my concerts and not to buy my records.

For a while the phone rang constantly, either with a reporter on the other end of the line asking pointed questions or with my agent or someone else bearing more bad news about the public's response. Ironically, a couple of the panicky calls were from the business and charitable agencies I had called earlier in the summer to confess and apologize to.

"When you said you'd had an inappropriate relationship with another man while you were married, we didn't realize you meant a *sexual* relationship!" one of the executives said.

"I honestly wasn't trying to hedge at all," I told him. "I was just trying to say it a little more gently. I thought you understood, but it looks like instead you were giving me the benefit of the doubt, thinking I would never have crossed *that* line. But I did. And I'm sorry. I apologize again, and I ask your forgiveness."

Across the board, my apologies to these agencies were accepted, but there was still a price to be paid. My affiliation with the charities was obviously causing them embarrassment, so I quickly resigned as their spokesperson. The same thing happened with the Young Messiah Tour; I would not be traveling with the familiar lineup of artists during the holiday season. My record label decided to postpone the release of my upcoming Christmas album.

In the midst of the mayhem of negative publicity, there were people in our church and in our town who reached out to show us love and understanding. One friend called me during that time and simply asked if I could watch her two boys for a couple of hours while she and her husband attended a meeting. In other times, it would have been just two moms exchanging baby-sitting favors. But in those turbulent days, I knew it was more than that. This was someone who was saying, without words, *Sandi, I know what the press is saying about you. But I know who you really are, and I'm entrusting my children to you.* What a powerful validation of our friendship that was for me!

And then there were those people I would encounter out in the supermarket or post office or at school events. While some would stare and then look away, others would step up to shake my hand or offer a hug and say, "Sandi, I just want you to know I'm thinking of you and remembering you in my prayers," or simply, "We love you, Sandi." Little incidents like that made those days a poignant and bittersweet time.

In some ways the situation seemed so ironic. In my personal life, I had come out of a fiery-furnace experience to find grace and happiness like I'd never known before. God had forgiven me; I knew that for sure. I was head-over-heels in love with my new husband, and our kids were settling in to form a large, boisterously happy family. I had found love, healing, and restoration through the patient, insightful workings of my godly home church.

I was ready to hit the road again, rested, rejuvenated, and re-born, eager to empower my music with a new understanding of God's bountiful mercy and wonderful grace. But suddenly nobody wanted me to come.

Looking back, one of the things that makes me the saddest, and one of the things I really wish could be understood, is that by the time my story hit the press and people began to hear what I had done, I had already been through a tremendous healing process with my family and my church. While it was obviously news to most people who were hearing about it, it wasn't as though it had just happened; there was a lot more to the story than was being told. Not that sin is ever old news, but my family was beginning to put the pieces back together again, and while I don't ever want to be critical of the media, it did make me sad that many of the writers chose to leave out the recovery part of my journey. For me, it's always been about the *whole* story: beginning, middle, and end. But too many times, only the beginning was told.

A Time for Reflection

In some ways the aftermath of the publicity firestorm was a mixed blessing. Yes, it hurt to be shunned and condemned by the

Christian community outside my home church. But because so many dates had been canceled, I had more time at home to adjust to my new role as wife and mother-in-residence to seven lively children.

On those days when Don was working at the Y, the kids were at school, and I found myself alone in the house, I often sang the hauntingly beautiful lyrics I had recorded two years earlier for the *Le Voyage* album. The songs commemorate the journey of a sojourner known as Traveler who chooses to follow her faithful Companion off the broad path and through the narrow gate. Her choice forces her to feel occasional desperation and fear but ultimately brings her to new heights of jubilation. That's exactly the dichotomy I felt during those quiet times: I was facing a bleak time in my career, yet I felt joyfully content and at peace—forgiven by my Savior and embraced by my family.

There was nothing left to do but enjoy that quiet, peaceful stage and make the most of being at home with Don and our children. I accepted the few bookings that trickled in, but the crowds were small and the response wasn't nearly as warm as it had been a couple of years earlier. I completely understood how disappointed in me and disillusioned the fans felt.

I compared it with going to a doctor I trusted and finding out that the doctor had done something totally and scandalously unethical. I would have some issue with that, because I would have some expectations about his behavior and his actions due to the MD he put behind his name. I would be disappointed and disillusioned and maybe even a little angry.

It's the same for me as a Christian artist, putting myself out there on the stage and attaching *Christian* to my name. When I do that, there is an expectation that I'm going to live by the guidelines found in God's Word. But I violated those guidelines; I didn't live up to my own commitment to live a Christlike life. So people were greatly disappointed in me. Even angry. I was learning firsthand that sin doesn't just hurt the sinner; it has the potential to hurt a lot of other people too. I had made some poor choices, and now I had to face the music, as the old saying goes.

The mail was an interesting assortment during those months when I was out of the spotlight. I got several letters of love and encouragement, saying things like, "I don't agree with your decisions, but I love and support you. Everybody makes mistakes." And there were lots of very harsh, hurtful letters in which the writers shared how disgusted they were by my behavior.

I tried to answer all of them, especially the ones I categorized as hate mail. "I understand how you feel. I know I let you down," I wrote back to them. "I'm sorry for the hurt and disappointment I've caused you."

Sometimes I got letters back from those people saying, "I don't feel any differently about your situation, but I'm sorry I lashed out at you out of my own hurt. I'll be praying for you, asking God to make Himself known to you in a very real, wonderful way."

He certainly did just that. What I learned from the ordeal we went through was that, once you get to the place where you surrender yourself to Him and become willing to do whatever it takes to make things right, God will pick up the pieces of your broken life and bless you in spite of the mistakes you've made.

Don and I aren't the first ones to see that happen, of course. To find an earlier example, you can read 2 Samuel 11–12, which recounts the sordid, heartbreaking story of David and Bathsheba, who was married to Uriah until David committed adultery with her and arranged to have Uriah killed in battle.

The anguish David and Bathsheba suffered because of their sin went far beyond anything Don and I had to endure, as bad as that seemed at the time. Their consequences included the death of their child. Surely there's nothing worse than that! After God exacted such a terrible price from David and Bathsheba, it seems completely unlikely that He would then bless them once they had been restored to Him through forgiveness and grace. But that's what He did. After their first child died, they quickly became the parents of another child, Solomon. And that's not all. The rest of the story is found on the opening page of the New Testament, which traces the genealogy of Jesus. There, in the list of the Messiah's earthly ancestors, are the two people you might least expect to find. In tracing the lineage of Jesus's earthly father, Joseph, verse 6 names "David . . . the father of Solomon, whose mother had been Uriah's wife."

> *God will pick up the pieces of your broken life and bless you in spite of the mistakes you've made.*

Does this say to us, then, that God willed that sin to happen so Solomon could be born and lead a line of descendants that would result in the Messiah? Absolutely not. God is *never* part of sin. But what this does say to me is that when we reach a place in our lives, as David did, where the impact of what we've done hits us and we fall on our face and cry out in repentance to our God, He is faithful to pick us up and give us a new beginning. And in that new life in Him, there are blessings. Solomon was one of those blessings.

Reading David's story and then understanding the rest of the story in Matthew 1, how could anyone doubt that our God is the God of second chances?

I paid a difficult price for the ugly mistakes I made in my life, but when I was restored to God, He blessed me despite my mistakes and wove together a beautiful family full of love and happiness to surround me.

I shouldn't have done things the way I did. I should have made so many different and better choices. But as I rode out the terrible consequences of my sin, I realized anew that God is the God of truth, and I constantly felt the increasing rewards of freedom as my ugly truth was made known. I had said to the world, "Here it is. I'm not proud of it, but here it is. I apologize for what I did. Now God has forgiven me and extended His grace over me, and I hope you can too."

Quiet Time

Over the next few months, Sandi Patty dropped off the radar of the Christian music world. It wasn't what I wanted, but under the circumstances, it was a good thing as I continued, in prayer and humility, with the steps toward restoration. And honestly, except for the abiding embarrassment over my mistakes and the regret that it had apparently taken away—or at least greatly curtailed— my career, I was happier than I had ever been. I adored being Don's wife, and I especially loved being, with just a rare travel appearance now and then, a stay-at-home mom. It was something I had often longed for but never had felt able to do while I was the sole support of my family and so many others.

It was a wonderful beginning to our new life together. In fact, Don and I were so enthralled, so completely delighted, with our large, energetic passel of charming and enjoyable children that occasionally we started having a recklessly crazy thought: *What if we added one more?*

Before you had a name, or opened up your eyes
Or anyone could recognize your face
You were being formed so delicate in size,
secluded in God's safe and hidden place.
Little tiny hands, and little tiny feet,
little eyes that shimmer like a pearl,
He breathed in you a song, and to make it all complete
He brought the masterpiece into the world.

—Brent Alan Henderson, Craig Patty, Michael Patty, and Gloria Gaither
"Masterpiece"

Chapter Ten

SAM

Occasionally, when we were sure no one was listening (probably for fear they would call the men in the white coats to take us off to a mental hospital), Don and I mused about how really special it would be to celebrate our marriage with the life of a little one, a baby that belonged to both of us. Then we would look around us, remember that we already had seven kids, and slap ourselves back into reality!

But another week or so would go by and, as crazy as it seemed, the topic would come up again. No sooner did we bring up the idea than we would shoot it down, quickly listing all the reasons why it was ridiculous to even consider such a wacko scheme. For starters, I had had my tubes tied, and the thought of going through the reversal procedure made me cringe. Also, I had already had three C-sections; to be honest, I just wasn't willing to put my body through that ordeal again.

"I totally agree," Don would say, nodding vigorously and patting my hand.

Then we thought of a different approach. Don had been adopted as an infant, and we both are very strongly pro-life. But we also believe Christians have to make a home for the babies we say should be born, so we're strongly pro-adoption too. Adoption, then, was something we might consider—in our more insane moments. Then we would move on once again, putting the issue aside and going back to the houseful of kids we already had.

One day, out of the blue, Don said to me, "You know, if we ever did decide to adopt a baby, it would be great to have a little boy and name him after my dad. You know, name him Sam."

Don's adoptive dad, Sam Peslis, had died when Don was just eleven years old. His adoptive mom had died when Don was in his twenties. His parents had provided him with a loving home, and I sensed that Don was feeling that by adopting a child he might, in some way, return the blessing he had been given.

But then the kids would act up, and that would jerk us back to our senses yet again. Really, we agreed, seven kids was *enough*.

One day, when I was alone, the thought popped into my head yet again, and I stopped what I was doing, closed my eyes, and prayed, in a rather exasperated tone, "God, if You want this to happen, You're just gonna have to drop a baby in our lap. Amen."

The Crazy Idea

We went on a cruise with Shari Schrock, one of my ya-ya girl-friends, and her husband, Wes, a local attorney. Their adopted son,

Ryan, is one of Anna's best friends. As close as we are, I had not told Shari—or anyone else—the crazy idea that kept popping into my private conversations with Don. But on the cruise, we talked a lot about their son's adoption and also about Don's adoption—not that we knew much about it.

After Don's adoptive mother died in 1987, he found in her safe-deposit box some papers that showed his birth mother's name and where he had been born. But he didn't know anything about his birth father, and he had been unsuccessful in finding anyone who knew his birth mother. He hadn't felt any particular urgency to get his questions answered. He would just occasionally send out a feeler, and when his efforts failed to turn up any information, he wasn't upset. "I always trusted God that I would know what I needed to know about my parents, and all in His timing," Don told our friends. "I haven't forced it. I haven't hired a detective. I've just found what information I could find, and I think when God says it's time for me to find them, I will."

"God, if You want this to happen, You're just gonna have to drop a baby in our lap. Amen."

We got home at the end of the week, in time for a Super Wind-Down with the kids that Friday night. We moved the furniture around as usual, hauled in pillows and sleeping bags, microwaved some popcorn, and prepared to camp out around the TV with a good movie. The kids always preferred to watch the new movies, something we had rented for the evening. But for some reason—and I still don't know where this movie came from—we watched *Yours, Mine, and Ours,* starring Henry Fonda and Lucille Ball. Perhaps you've seen this wonderful classic about a blended family—and a new baby. It was a fun night.

On Saturday morning I was working in the kitchen when the phone rang. It was Shari, and she seemed a little rattled. "Sandi, I don't even know why I'm calling you," she began. "But this baby has been born . . ."

I stopped what I was doing and sat down on a stool at the breakfast bar. My heart took a strange little leap.

"Wes is handling an adoption, and the people who were going to adopt this baby—well, the adoption has fallen through." Shari's words came gushing through the cordless phone like water shooting out of a firefighter's hose. "We've called everybody we can think of—the judge, the adoption agencies in this area—and nothing has worked out. Now we're running out of time; if the baby isn't adopted within twenty-four hours, it has to go into the foster-care system. So we're just calling everyone we know to see if anyone knows anybody who is looking to adopt. You don't know anyone, do you?"

Finally she stopped, and the phone went silent.

"Sandi? Are you there?"

It's a cliché, I know, but time stood still. Somehow I had lost my voice.

"Sandi?"

I answered slowly, "Shari, *we* might be."

"Oh, give me a break!" she said. "Are you kidding? Sandi, you've already got seven kids!"

"No, listen," I said. "Don and I have been talking . . ." I walked her through our secret conversations, and I added, "We've thought about adopting and how meaningful that would be for Don. We had thought it would be really special if it were a boy—"

"Oh! It's a boy!" Shari squealed.

"—and we'd name him Sam, after Don's dad," I finished.

The line between us was quiet once more. Finally I said, "I need to talk to Don. I'll call you back."

The funny thing was, right before Shari called me, she had been pacing back and forth in her own kitchen, arguing with God: "I'm *not* calling Sandi, Lord. She's already got seven kids. I'm not bothering her with this."

She told me later, "I finally had to call you to get God off my back!"

Since it was Saturday, Don was home. I repeated the little bit of information I had gotten from Shari about the baby. Then I told him about my exasperated prayer several weeks earlier. For a moment all we could do was stand there and look at each other. Could this be God dropping a baby in our lap?

All the reasons why it was ridiculous for us to bring another child into our family were still there, every one of them. The only thing that seemed to argue against anything on the list was that flippant little prayer.

Looking for someone who might make sense of what was happening, we got on two extension phones and called Pastor Lyon. We should have known better. Pastor Lyon is an adopted son. "If you're looking for a rational decision, you're not going to get it from me," he said with a warm laugh. "This is a baby who needs a home, and obviously God has opened this door for you."

We talked a little more, telling him about the twenty-four-hour deadline. He said, "If another family comes forward, maybe that's what's supposed to happen. But if not, maybe this *is* God dropping a baby into your lap. Maybe this is your fleece."

He was referring to a story in the Old Testament book of Judges (6:36–40) that describes how Gideon used a wool fleece as a way for God to verify his intentions to Gideon:

> Gideon said to God, "If you will save Israel by my hand as you have promised—look, I will place a wool fleece on the threshing floor. If there is dew only on the fleece and all the ground is dry, then I will know that you will save Israel by my hand, as you said." And that is what happened. Gideon rose early the next day; he squeezed the fleece and wrung out the dew—a bowlful of water.

> Then Gideon said to God, "Do not be angry with me. Let me make just one more request. Allow me one more test with the fleece. This time make the fleece dry and the ground covered with dew." That night God did so. Only the fleece was dry; all the ground was covered with dew.

We called the kids together for a family meeting. As soon as we said "baby," they all got really, really quiet—especially Erin, my youngest. She looked at me with sad eyes and said, "Mom, I always wanted to be your last baby." Then we explained that we were considering *adopting* a baby, and she said, "Oh! OK, that's fine." The other kids immediately agreed, and we all started daydreaming about what it would be like to have a baby in the house. "Maybe we could make that little room into a nursery," somebody said. Then the boys offered to let the baby sleep with them. One of the girls pointed out, rather wistfully, that "it would be just like that movie we watched last night."

Good job, God! I silently prayed. I still didn't know where the old video had come from—but I had a good idea who had been behind our watching it!

We explained to the kids that we were going to wait and see if another family came forward within the twenty-four-hour time limit, and if no one did, we would consider strongly that God was moving us in that direction. Everyone was blabbing at once, excitedly sharing ideas and opinions. Suddenly Jonathan, who was eight at the time, piped up. "Mom, we just need to pray for one of those blankets," he said.

He meant a fleece. Obviously, we were all thinking alike!

Not Just Any Ol' Burning Bush

I called Betty Fair, our beloved nanny. Her son and daughter-in-law had adopted a child a couple of years earlier, and I asked if she would call them and ask if they might be interested in this baby. She did. But her daughter-in-law had gotten pregnant soon after they adopted, so they already had a toddler and an infant to care for. Sadly, they had to say no.

I asked Betty what she would think if we adopted the baby. The line seemed to go dead.

"Betty, are you there?"

"It hits me cold, Sandi. Real cold," said this woman who was spending a great deal of time with our family, trying to shepherd our small army of active youngsters and keep the household running. "You know, you already have *seven* children."

Betty's reaction has become a standard line at our house now whenever something seems like an idea that has come from another planet: "It hits me cold," we say ominously. "Real cold."

Laughter always follows, because we all know that today Betty, like the rest of us, can't imagine life without the little guy we were about to welcome into our hearts.

Next I called my parents, who were vacationing in Hawaii after completing a music tour in California. They too were quiet after I told them what we were considering. It was as though something in the phone line made it go dead each time the preposterous idea was uttered.

"Sandi, you know we're behind you 100 percent. We'll support you whatever you decide," Mom said. "But, honey, you know, you already have *seven* kids."

"Yeah, Mom," I answered. "That's what everybody keeps telling us."

The day dragged by. All we could think about was the little baby just a couple of blocks away in the hospital nursery, waiting for a home. For Don, it was an especially meaningful day; he couldn't help but think of that baby and see himself as an infant thirty-five years earlier, waiting in a hospital nursery for an unknown family to take him home.

Sunday morning came, and we skipped church. The deadline was approaching; a decision had to be made. Again Don and I went through the list of why it was foolish to consider adding an eighth child to our flock. Then I laughed and said to him, "You *know* we're supposed to do this."

"Yeah," he answered. "I do." And then back we flipped, to the other side of the argument. Of course we couldn't have another child!

Wes and Shari came over about 11 a.m., bringing with them a box of Dunkin' Donuts. Shari, who's usually very mystical and sees meaning in everything that happens, was determined to talk us out of our silly notion. Wes, on the other hand, who's always very analytical and practical, set those donuts down and said, "I'm here to tell you, I've heard from the Lord, and you are supposed to have this baby."

"Wes!" Shari scolded.

We started going through the pros and cons yet again. Finally I said, "Wes, all morning, all I've been able to think was that I have to go see this baby. Is that possible?"

Wes made some phone calls, then we climbed into their car for the short drive to the hospital. Before we started into the building, Shari grabbed our hands and said, "OK, God. We need You involved in this. We need You *very* involved in this. In fact, we need a burning bush—and not just *any* ol' burning bush, but a smack-you-in-the-face burning bush. Don't be subtle, Lord!"

The deadline was approaching; a decision had to be made.

We made our way upstairs. Don and I waited in a small lobby while Wes and Shari went to get the baby. Soon we heard the wheels rattling as the cart was pushed down the hallway toward us. They turned the corner, and I was surprised to see that Shari was crying, alternately pressing her hand tightly against her mouth and then waving it toward the little clear-acrylic bassinet. She shook her head, unable to speak.

Oh, dear God. Something's wrong with the baby! I realized. Wes had told us there had been some major trouble in the delivery room. Now it seemed that more unexpected problems had occurred.

They pushed the crib nearer, and I could see the tiny, bundled life inside: the most beautiful four-pound, eleven-ounce, tawny-skinned, fuzzy-haired baby I'd ever seen. Then I noticed that, above the baby's tiny head, a heart-shaped piece of paper had been taped to the bassinet. A rainbow had been colored onto the top of the heart, and something was written underneath.

The paper was the cause of Shari's tears. It was a nametag.

"The nurses . . . named him . . . when he was born," she finally managed to push out, in between gulps and sniffs.

We stooped and squinted to read the heart-shaped paper.

The baby's name was Sam.

If home is really where the heart is,
Then home must be a place that we all can share,
For even with our differences our hearts are much the same,
For where love is, we come together there.
Wherever there is laughter ringing,
Someone smiling, someone dreaming,
We can live together there,
Love will be our home.
—Steven Curtis Chapman
"Love Will Be Our Home"

Chapter Eleven

THE ALMOSTS

Tearing through the Super Target store Sunday evening with the whole tribe in tow, we filled several carts with diapers, blankets, baby clothes, bedding, bottles, formula, a crib, a stroller, and enough other stuff to keep Sam decked out in grand style until at least his twenty-second birthday.

Anderson is a pretty small town, and a lot of people know us. Don and I had been married only six months, and I'm sure more than one of our fellow shoppers that evening eyed all the baby stuff in our baskets, remembered the scandal that had brought us together, and thought, *So that's why they got married!*

The cashier's eyebrows shot up when we steered our caravan of carts into her lane. "Wow!" she said, probably wishing she worked on commission.

"We're adopting a baby tomorrow!" one of the kids explained.

We were in a tizzy most of the night, getting everything ready. I don't know about Don, but I didn't sleep for one measly moment. We were so keyed up, so excited, you would have thought we were first-time parents about to go into labor. And once more, our experience gave Don insights into his own past. As we eagerly rearranged our lives to welcome this child into our midst, Don's thoughts flew back four decades to imagine his own adoptive parents, excitedly preparing to bring him home.

At the hospital the next day, there was lots of paperwork, but Wes was there to help us work our way through it. We were doing OK until we came to a question on one of the first forms that we didn't know how to answer. The question asked for the baby's race. Sam is multiracial—his birth parents were biracial, so he has a wonderfully diverse pool of African American, Native Indian, and Caucasian genes. So we looked at that question and were stumped for an answer. Finally I took the pen from Don and said, "Here. I know what to say."

Now we were more than yours and mine. We had an ours too.

On the blank beside the word *Race*, I wrote, "HUMAN." It has become our standard response to the question anytime it's asked.

And then he was there, in our arms and in our hearts, one of us forever and ever. It felt wonderful to walk around the house with a sweet little newborn in my arms—without the stiffness and pain of recovering from yet another Cesarean section. We spent every moment we could bonding with our little Sam.

He didn't sleep well at first, but that didn't matter. As soon as he would hiccup or cough or make the tiniest little squeak of a noise, someone would rush to scoop him up and settle into the rocking chair for some serious cuddling and cooing. I don't think he spent more than ten minutes in his brand-new crib that first day. He was too cute to put down: irresistibly sweet, an undeniable godsend. Later I would look at Don lying on the bed or on the floor with little Sam sleeping on his chest, and my heart would melt. Suddenly neither of us could remember a single thing on that long list of negatives we'd gone through so many times in the previous weeks and months. What were we thinking? Of *course* we needed this baby!

Another Road Dog

It's funny how one week of your life can be so totally, wonderfully different from the one before. On Friday we had been a happy, blended family of nine with no idea the weekend would bring anything but the normal routine. But on Monday our home was happily hijacked by a four-pound, eleven-ounce little boy who stole our hearts and brought a whole new dimension of joy to our family. Now we were more than *yours* and *mine*. We had an *ours* too.

Things happened so quickly that most of our friends and neighbors were caught completely off guard by this turn of events. When my manager called late Monday morning, as he did each Monday to touch base as the week began, Don's son, Donnie, answered the phone and told him, "Just a minute. I'll get Sandi. She's changing our new baby."

When I came on the line, my manager said, "Sandi, I must have misunderstood. It sounded like Donnie said you had a new baby?"

I had to laugh, thinking it was going to be a fun week as all our friends and business contacts heard the news. The manager reminded me of the concert I had scheduled the next weekend in Evansville, and I quipped cheerfully, "I'll be there. We'll bring Sam!" During that slow period in my career, I wasn't about to turn down any bookings.

By the next Saturday morning, when we took little Sam to Donnie and Jonathan's basketball game, we had learned to reduce our loading time for getting all the kids and baby gear into vehicles (think *caravan* rather than *car*), ready for transport, to less than twenty-five minutes. It wasn't quite as quick as, say, fire-department standards, but for the ten of us, it seemed like a major accomplishment.

That was about the time I started thinking of our family as "The Almosts" because, in so many undertakings, we *almost* get things right. Or we *almost* get somewhere on time. A typical "almost" occurred when I had a decorative artist paint a personalized border on the walls around our breakfast nook. She painted a wild array of beautiful flowers, swirls, and curlicues, and wove among them the "fruit of the spirit," as found in Galatians 5:22–23, along with all of our names. I wrote down the list of names and "fruit" for the painter—love, joy, peace, patience, kindness, faithfulness, gentleness, and self-control—and when she finished we all stood back in awe of her excellent work and my creative idea. Then one of the kids said, "Mom, you forgot *goodness*!" We *almost* got it right. So the painter had to come back and add *goodness* in an almost-perfect spot.

But in Sam there was no "almost." In our eyes he was perfect in every way.

He was ten days old and weighed less than five pounds when he made his first appearance at the basketball court, and he's been an athlete ever since. We took him to Donnie and Jonathan's game the first Saturday we had him, and that afternoon, Don and I packed up all the baby gear again and headed to Evansville to introduce him to the other thing that would be a familiar element in his life: a concert with Mom. That time we were off to Evansville for a pops concert with the symphony there.

A little earlier in that time of involuntary leisure in my career, the local symphony in Anderson had invited me to do a pops concert with them. It was something different for me, but I agreed to do it. As I said, I wasn't turning down any booking invitations during that time. And besides, a pops concert would be fun. "It sounds like a blast," I replied enthusiastically.

Anderson is small, but it has a very good symphony orchestra, and the concert—a great lineup of show tunes and patriotic music—had gone over very well. The response was warm and enthusiastic, but honestly, I thought that would be the end of it. Instead, a couple of other symphonies heard about the concert and invited me to sing with them too; one of them was in Evansville. I didn't realize it at the time, but God was opening a door to what would become a rewarding second phase of my music career. Since then I've sung with symphonies in many other cities, from Atlanta, Boston, and Louisville to Cincinnati, Dallas, and Houston.

But of course I didn't know the upcoming performance in Evansville was another step toward a new stage in my life. I was simply happy to be heading off to sing again and to be taking my husband and new baby along with me. Don and I packed up all the baby paraphernalia, left the rest of the kids in Betty's expert care, and took Sam on the road with us. He was a great little traveler, and Don is the best-ever stage dad. While I was out in the spotlight, the two of them were bonding behind the scenes.

What a happy time that was for all of us. We loved watching Sam gain new skills and awareness each day. He fit right into our on-the-go family and seemed to love being with us, whether we were at home, on the road, or flitting from one church- or school-related activity to another. Oh, sure, there were some down times. While my appearances with symphonies were popular and fun, the few dates when I appeared in churches were not always as pleasant.

He found me there on the back row and brought me back from the brink, and He can find you too.

Sometimes the church was less than half full. Sometimes the applause was short and muted. Sometimes I sat at the autograph table, idly tapping my pen and smiling as the crowds hurried out the door without stopping.

But all those imperfect moments quickly vanished when I was welcomed home by my handsome, adoring husband and our happy houseful of children. What a special day it was when Sam rewarded me for my performance as a mother with his first smile. If I'd had to, I would have given up all the awards I'd ever received to get to that moment; how blessed I was that God gave it to me for free.

Sam not only bonded quickly with his parents and siblings; he was also quickly accepted into the family by our little mutt, Brownie, a feisty, now–thirteen-year-old, fun-loving canine who thinks he owns the place. Whenever we would spread a blanket on the floor to let Sam kick and coo in the midst of the family, Brownie would sidle up to him, lie down beside him protectively—and growl at anyone who came close.

Sam was about a month old when his dedication service was held at our church. Standing there in front of the congregation that day, joyfully and gratefully holding my precious child in my arms, I couldn't help but think how we had sat on that front row less than a year earlier, filled with shame and humility as we stood before the church. How good God was—and is—to bring us back to that same place so we could share this wonderful blessing of joy with our church friends. As we joined Pastor Lyon at the front of the church and handed Sam over to him, I happened to glance upward, toward the back of the church.

Toward the balcony.

I remembered the baby dedication I had witnessed the first time I'd come to North Anderson, remembered crying as the parents renewed their commitment to God and to each other. I couldn't make out the faces of the people sitting up there near the top, the ones bathed in the muted colors washing down from the big, stained-glass window. I wondered if one of them was sitting up there crying, broken on the back row, as I had been. *God bless you,* I prayed silently, in a split-second rush. *He hasn't forgotten about you. He is the God of grace, the God of second chances and new beginnings. He found me there on the back row and brought me back from the brink, and He can find you too.*

CHAPTER ELEVEN

Our Cast of Characters

Our family was blessed by little Sam's arrival, but we had a lot of good things going for us even before he came along. Let me take a moment to introduce you to this wonderful cast of characters.

Don. My sweetheart and best friend, Don is the best husband and greatest dad any family could ever dream of sharing a life with. He is funny, considerate, kind, and oh, so romantic. When I've been away on a trip, I call him on the cell phone as I'm driving home from the airport, and when I arrive, he's usually standing in the driveway to greet me. I spring out of the car and fall into his embrace as though I've just come home from a twenty-year exile. It seems almost too good to be true sometimes, but Don has a wonderful way of making me feel like the sexiest, smartest, funniest, most beautiful and desirable woman in the world. How blessed I am to have him as my husband and lifetime companion.

Anna. I've already told you about my oldest wonder child, Anna. Soon to be twenty-one, she has logged more miles and accompanied me to more countries than any of the other kids, primarily because she's been around longer to do it. Anna grew up knowing what it was like to wake up in the morning and have no idea where she was—and to not give it another thought as long as she was near me. We've spent so much time on the road together that today she serves as something like a junior road manager for me—and for our family. Whenever the whole clan is going somewhere together for a vacation or some other trip—quite an undertaking, as you might imagine—Anna's the one who books the flights, gets the rental cars, and makes the hotel reservations. Having studied dance all her life (she's also taught dance for several years), she is a gifted ballerina, and I love bringing her along with me to concerts whenever we can arrange it. We do a song together—I sing, she dances—and it's a beautiful moment.

Recently Anna, a college junior, moved into a house near campus with four other girls. It's not all that far from our house, but it marked a transition in our relationship. Now that she's in a house instead of the dorm, it feels more like she has her own home, and she won't be coming here as much to spend days at a time during the holidays or to do her laundry or watch something special on cable TV. As I helped her pack for the move, I felt a little melancholy, remembering all the times during the last twenty years when I had packed for her or helped her pack. She's been traveling with me since she was six weeks old; I remember those cute little baby clothes and that mountain of baby paraphernalia I took along to England for her first Billy Graham Crusade, and all the sizes of outfits I packed for her through the years. Sweet memories . . . and more to come, I'm sure.

Jennifer. One of my twins, seventeen-year-old Jenni is as comfortable in the spotlight as any seasoned performer. She shares the stage with me as a guest artist, whenever her schedule allows it, on the Hymns of Faith Tour. She has a wonderful voice—and I'm not the only one who holds that opinion. Like most of the other kids in our family, she is very active in her high school's show choir, a competitive musical ensemble that last year was selected to go to the national competition in Orlando. In addition to that honor, Jenni was selected to compete at the national level as a soloist. And guess who she asked to accompany her on the piano: Mom.

Taking our place before the judges during the final round, I don't know who was more nervous—Jenni or me. She was the first of the three finalists to sing, and as she started, there was something wrong with the microphone. But she kept on going for a verse and chorus, as calm and cool as though she were singing in the shower. I, on the other hand, was firing off death-ray looks toward the audio people while I was playing the piano. Finally, thankfully, they stopped her and gave her a new microphone. Jenni was such a pro. She just smiled and started over from the top, singing Rachel Lampa's song "No Greater Love." When she was done, the whole gym full of people gave her a standing ovation. And then—what a thrill!—at the end of the evening they named her the winner and gave her a trophy half the size of Sam.

Jonathan can flat-out perform, and no one loves seeing him do it more than his mom.

As I was finishing this book, Jenni was invited to do her first performance for pay—as we call it, her first "paid gig." She was asked to sing during a large youth rally in Louisville, and as she was rushing to leave for her big night (her dad was driving her down there), she suddenly turned and said, "Oh! Mom! Do I need earrings?"

"Yes, my darling!" I answered with a laugh and yanked off the ones I was wearing. "Here you go! Now you have *everything* you need."

By all accounts, her debut was a smash hit.

Jonathan. Jenni's twin brother, Jonathan, may be the most naturally musical member of the family. He has what's called "relative perfect pitch." Here's what that means: People who have true perfect pitch cannot change key; when they're singing a cappella with a group, it's almost inevitable for the group to stray off key, especially a young group like the high-schoolers Jonathan sings with in show choir. They're just gonna go a little flat; it's to be expected. But when you have perfect pitch, you can't go off key with everyone else, which leaves you hanging out there sounding out of tune with everybody else. When Jonathan sings a cappella with the madrigals, the group goes flat, and it makes him crazy. But the important thing is that he can "adjust his head" and go along with them so the whole group still sounds harmonious. There's not one lone voice sticking out there that's still on key but actually sounds off key.

Jonathan's a little shy and enjoys his own company; he can spend hours happily reading or messing around with the computer. But an amazing thing happens when he steps out into the spotlight. He absolutely blossoms. It's an incredible transformation, something akin to quiet, shy Clark Kent changing clothes and becoming Superman. Jonathan can flat-out perform, and no one loves seeing him do it more than his mom.

Donnie. The comedian of the family, Don's sixteen-year-old son, Donnie, happily takes credit for teaching me everything I know about sarcasm. He also claims to have first "met" Jonathan, then his classmate, when he (Donnie) was establishing himself as chief dynamo on the second-grade playground. If there's a funny or clever way to look at a familiar situation, we can count on Donnie to see it first. He went through a demanding transition with humor and patience when Don and I blended our families. Accustomed to being the oldest child, Donnie suddenly found himself one of three kids who were tied for the middle spot.

Donnie is also blessed with an abundance of musical talent, and in my totally biased opinion, he, Jonathan, and Jenni are the hands-down best members of their high-school show choir. This year they have been joined by Aly, so now they're the four best members. Donnie has a great voice and great imagination, so he's wonderfully creative in all sorts of musical roles.

Aly. Don's older daughter is now fifteen and learning to drive. She is smart and beautiful and also is learning to play the guitar. What a gracious and kind personality she has. When Don and I were first married, she and her sister, Mollie, shared a room with Erin—three girls sharing a bedroom, and until we moved into our new house, the three of them also had to share a bathroom with Anna and Jenni. Let me tell you, that took some planning; scheduling showers and mirror time was like planning takeoffs and arrivals at LAX. But Aly worked through the transition as though it were perfectly natural to go from a "normal" family with three kids to a blended family with seven (or more).

She's a delightful young woman, and she has an amazing resemblance to her grandmother; I'll tell you more about that a little later. One of the funny stories we tell about Aly concerns her happy disposition. She is constantly humming and singing little songs to herself, merrily moving through the day. When she was little, she was humming at school one day, and her friend sighed in exasperation and said, "Aly, that humming is really getting on my nerves. Could you please be quiet?"

Aly, equally exasperated, replied, "I know. It's getting on my nerves too, but I can't stop."

Erin. My "baby," Erin is now fifteen and also learning to drive. (That's right, folks: this year we have *five* teenage drivers and student drivers in this family. My advice is that you might want to stay off those Indiana highways for a while.) Erin seems to be skipping the unpleasant adolescent-to-teenage stage and going straight to the joyful, fun-to-be-with years. She didn't have nearly as much time on the tour bus as the rest of the kids, so today when she comes with me, it's as though she's discovering all the fun to be had for the first time. She's always flitting around, discovering something new in a familiar thing. The family's favorite Erin-ism came as the twins were preparing for baptism. We were all sitting around, discussing what it meant to give your life to Jesus and how exciting it was that they were taking the step of being baptized. Erin, then a sweet little grade-schooler, sighed and said, "Mommy, I wanna be appetized too."

Erin has entered high school and is into the show-choir thing at her school, which is different from the other kids' high school. We live in a small town, yet we have two high schools, and Erin, always wanting to make her own path, decided she wanted to go to the other one. So she is now in the rival show choir that competes against Jenni, Donnie, Jonathan, and Aly's show choir, which sparks some interesting conversations among the kids. Don and I just get out of the way—unless, of course, blood is drawn. Then they're all grounded. Whew! Sometimes I wish somebody would ground *me* and send me to *my* room . . . alone!

Mollie. When our families blended, Erin relinquished to Don's sweet little Mollie her spot as the baby of the family, although they both tend to share the position if there's something in it for them. Mollie is a thoughtful, caring, outward-focused girl of thirteen, an angel on earth. While Don and his former wife agreed that it would be better for the kids to stay in their hometown and live with Don full time, Mollie has chosen to live with her mother during the past year, in part because she wanted to support her mom as she began her battle with cancer. Mollie knew no one could encourage her mom and lift her spirits like she could, and she wanted to be there to walk that challenging path side by side with her. That's the kind of wonderful young woman she is.

One of my favorite Mollie stories took place at our wedding reception. When we got back from Estes Park, several of our friends threw us a wonderful wedding reception. Our friends and lots of our kids' friends were invited. Mollie, who was three then, was the cutest little peanut at the party. She was at an age that, whenever she got tired, she would curl up on the lap of anyone who was close and fall asleep. That night she curled up on my dad's lap—we all call him Papa—and fell asleep on his shoulder. Papa has always had a good shoulder for sweet moments as well as the sad ones. (I should know. I've used it a lot myself.)

He looked at us with an almost doleful expression and asked, "Why don't I have any stepparents?"

Sam. From the moment we brought Sam home, he has been *ours*. As I like to say, he belongs to all of us, and we do our best to share him, but he's so darn cute it's difficult sometimes. Unlike the other kids, who have had to make transitions into this wild and crazy blended family, Sam has grown up seeing his brothers and sisters have two sets of parents. One summer when he was really little, my kids were heading off to their dad's house to spend some time there, and Don's kids were heading for their mom's house for a couple of weeks. Sam looked around the empty house, wondering where everyone had gone and why he was stuck here alone with Mom and Dad when his brothers and sisters were off having fun somewhere else. He looked at Mom and Dad with an almost doleful expression and asked, as though he were deprived, "Why don't *I* have any stepparents?"

Oh, the explaining we've had to do!

When I was out on the road alone recently, I called home and he said, with a bit of a whine in his voice, "Mom, why can't you have a job like other moms so you can stay home with me?" *Gulp*. I decided right then and there that I would bring him with me to my next concert.

I usually do travel with at least one of the kids whenever it works out for our schedules, and I decided it was Sam's turn for some road time with Mom. So Don met me in Fort Wayne, and Sam joined me on the bus. After the next concert, we drove from Columbus, Ohio, to Toledo and got to the hotel at about 2 a.m. Sam thought he wanted to watch a movie, so, trying to be a fun mom, I said sure, knowing he would go right to sleep. NOT! When I woke up at 4 a.m., Sam said, "Mom, you missed the best part." He cracks me up. He is definitely a road dog.

One Family, One Nickname

OK, that completes the introductions. Now let me tell you the story of our family's nickname. During the first summer after the wedding, we took a family vacation to Myrtle Beach. It was there that we came up with a new family name—or rather, a nickname. But it didn't come easily.

One day as we were leaving to go to the next activity, whatever it was, Don accidentally set off an explosion of emotions among the kids by calling, in his usual bright and cheery way, "Let's go, Peslis family!"

Without even knowing it, he triggered a knock-down-drag-out round of screaming and yelling—OK, it wasn't that bad, but things were pretty hot. The problem was that my four kids have always been Helverings, because that's their dad's last name. No way they wanted to change their name, and they wanted that fact to be recognized. Then they pointed out that they were also a family of Pattys because I had continued to use my maiden name professionally. And of course they insisted that our family includes their Nana and Papa Patty as well.

We stopped what we were doing and sat down for a family meeting. This problem was something we'd never thought about at all, and it obviously needed some real attention.

All the kids were invited to express their thoughts and ideas about the situation and what we should do. (It was unlikely that Don could remember to say, "Let's go, Peslis family and Helvering family and Patty family" every time we were trying to get somewhere.) First we thought about taking different parts of each name and putting them together: *Hel* from Helvering, *P* from Patty, and *Lis* from Peslis. But that left us with *Helplis*, and that just hit a little too close to home.

Finally it was decided that we would write the letters in the names on slips of paper and draw them out of a hat and try to use the letters to create a family nickname that would work for all of us. Eventually we came up with a name we have claimed and loved ever since (although we still have trouble with the spelling sometimes). Ladies and gentlemen, I introduce you to . . . the Ganisilapivy family.

Primetime

Life was good. I wasn't as busy professionally as I would have liked, but that just gave me more time to spend at home. In 1996 the postponed Christmas album, *O Holy Night!* was finally released, and I supported it with a Christmas tour, which did well and was warmly received. The next October, my record label released *Artist of My Soul,* and to my surprise it was a top-ten hit in the contemporary Christian music market for more than five weeks. Maybe, just maybe, I had turned a corner. Maybe, just maybe, the public had finally forgiven me for my mistakes.

I was feeling encouraged and almost confident when, out of the blue, an ABC News staffer called and proposed a segment on *Primetime,* the network's weekly news magazine. Naive me, I thought the show was looking for a story about the joys and challenges of blending two parents and a bunch of kids into one large, cohesive family.

So we welcomed the New York–based news crew into our home and let them shadow the kids as they went to school and hung out with their friends. The producer interviewed Don and me as the photographers followed all of us around. And although they asked a lot of questions about the divorce and the affair, it seemed like a very slight interest compared with all the time they spent filming our everyday routines. We all found it rather entertaining to have the newspeople underfoot as we went through the lighthearted daily business of being the Ganisilapivys.

The kids were excited about all the attention, especially Anna, who was thirteen then and happily setting off to the first day of eighth grade when the news crew showed up. Her friends noticed the cameras, of course, and excitedly insisted that Anna tell them when it was going to be aired. After all, they might be shown on national TV too.

Because of breaking news and other delays, the program didn't run for quite a while. But that gave the local press time to get wind of it so that when it was finally scheduled, it was promoted throughout our area. I was out of town on the Christmas tour the night it was broadcast and didn't even see the program when it first aired.

When she picked up the phone, there was a chill in her tone, a distance in her voice that I'd never heard before.

Anna remembers that night vividly. During those years she was really into dance and was at the dance school every night of the week except Friday and Sunday, so she wasn't home at the time of the broadcast. It was my kids' time to stay with their dad, and when Anna came home from dance class, she immediately sensed that something was wrong.

"The house was quiet when I walked in," she said, "and something seemed odd."

"What's going on?" she asked. "Why is everyone being so weird?"

"Sit down," her dad told her. "I need to talk to you."

He told her that the *Primetime* program had aired and that it wasn't what everyone had been expecting. Then he played the videotape he had made of it. The piece had almost nothing to do with our family. Instead it made an odd comparison between another Christian entertainer and me and the "issues" in our lives as Christian artists. The main "issue" in the interview with the other entertainer was that she had expanded her musical offerings and crossed over from contemporary Christian music to secular and had recently had a number-one hit song on the pop music charts.

As you might guess, my "issue" was a little more controversial. But just as I had done in every interview since that night on the floor of the Cleveland airport, I answered the reporter's questions with the whole, ugly truth, saying things like, "I don't want to pretend anymore. I want to set things right. I don't know if there's even a way to make some horrendous wrongs right."

The reporter explained in a voiceover, "Trapped in what she says was a loveless marriage, Sandi Patty began having an affair . . . with her backup singer, Don Peslis."

Sitting beside her dad and stepmother, Anna was stunned. While it had seemed to me that the whole wide world knew about the terrible sin I had committed, my own kids hadn't known, or at least they hadn't understood. They hadn't known Don and I had had an affair while I was still married to their father.

Now all the anguish of the scandal came rushing out again, but this time it wasn't happening in the world around us; it was directly hurting our children. When I found out what had happened, I rushed to call Anna, but when she picked up the phone, there was a chill in her tone, a distance in her voice that I'd never heard before.

"Sugar, I'm sorry. I thought you knew. We talked and talked and talked about all this. I thought you understood," I said.

"No, Mom, I *didn't* understand!" she sobbed. "I *didn't* know. You *didn't* tell me."

All the kids were hurt and humiliated by the program. After all, they had urged their friends to watch. And there were Don and I, being publicly scourged as Christian entertainers who had been committing adultery even as we sang about the glory and goodness of the Lord.

Anna bore the brunt of the pain because she was the oldest. She felt not only embarrassed and disgraced but also betrayed—by her own mother.

We were both in tears as we ended the call. I sat in my dressing room and cried, praying, *Lord, forgive me again for the things I have done, the mistakes I have made, the pain I have caused. Be with Anna now, Father. Hold her and help her. Keep her strong, and most of all tonight, help her feel my love—and Yours.*

The scene at Anna's school the next day was like "something out of a movie," she said later. "I felt like everyone was staring at me as I walked by, talking about me behind my back. One of my friends came up to me and asked, 'Are you OK?' Then another friend passed me a note, asking the same thing. They were supportive and understanding of what I was going through, but it was all just a little too much for me to handle that day."

Anna's teachers also tried to express support, although some of them were more hurtful than helpful. Finally Anna retreated to the choir room and asked her favorite teacher if she could stay there awhile to hide from all the staring eyes.

Things were a little uneasy between Anna and me for a week or so. The chill didn't last long, but it was certainly longer than we'd ever been at odds with each other before.

What had happened had made perfect sense at the time. Anna had been in second grade when I had separated from her father. Through the next couple of years I had talked with my kids many times about the divorce and how their father and I still loved them with all our hearts but that we just couldn't be married anymore. Don had done the same thing with his kids. In what we thought was an age-appropriate way—after all, they were still very young—we had gently told them about our feelings for each other and how we'd become friends and then that we had fallen in love with each other. To us it seemed we had told them and told them and told them and talked and talked and talked, but we had never used the adult words that they (and all their friends) heard that evening on national television. We didn't say, "We had an affair" and explain what that meant.

Even though the younger ones still didn't quite get the picture, they knew that, to the rest of the world, especially the Christian world, what their parents had done was very, very bad.

As soon as I got home from the tour I took the kids—and the video of the *Primetime* broadcast—to Pastor Lyon's office, and we all watched it again together. At the end of it, the pastor gently asked if they understood what the story had said about their mom. While Anna had gotten the message loud and clear, the twins, who were then ten, and Erin, who was just seven, were still pretty much in the dark. I took another shot at explaining it to them: "Well, it would be like . . . if Jenni had a boyfriend, and without breaking up with that boyfriend, she got another boyfriend."

Jenni's head shot up. "Oh, I would never do that! That wouldn't be right!"

That was the critical moment when it dawned on the young ones, *Oh, that's what happened.* They suddenly got it. And although it wasn't pretty, they felt better knowing that they now had the same facts the rest of the world had; they felt included and not left out.

I had learned yet another painful lesson: I would keep talking to my kids, keep the communication lines open, tell them as they grew older what I had told them when they were younger but with an ever-increasing tone of maturity.

While I had sought and received forgiveness, been restored to my church, and been blessed with a wonderful new life, the *Primetime* experience demonstrated the truth of a letter my church had sent out in response to press inquiries. The letter said, in part, "[Sandi] carries a sense of shame and a 'scarlet letter' (albeit self-imposed) that will haunt her as long as she lives."

A dad, timidly anxious to open a door,
A small boy inside without end,
Overwhelming and daunting from the start,
Both stayed true to the heart.
A few endeavors are meant to be,
God had a plan for you and me!
Once separated and unknown,
Now connected forever
On a journey of our own.

—Jim Perry, for his son Don Peslis
(with the help of his precious niece Barbie)

Chapter Twelve

A MOTHER LOST,
A FATHER FOUND

So far this book has been all about me. But I'd like to take a moment now to tell you a wonderful story about the man I love. It all began with an e-mail that appeared on my computer one morning in January 2004.

The e-mail message began with questions that made me gasp: "Is your husband Don? Was he born in West Virginia?"

My mouth fell open as I read the next words: "I may have info about his birth family. My maiden name was McGinnis." The writer included a phone number, and I hurriedly called Don at work to pass it along. "This might be it, sugar," I told him.

Don and I had been married nearly nine years, and during that time our love and happiness had expanded and evolved more than we could ever have imagined. In many ways, after its publicity-pounded beginning, our marriage still seemed like a dream come true. We had moved into a new house, and our wild and won-derful kids—who at that time were 20, 16, 16, 16, 15, 14, 12, and 8—were healthy, happy, and fun to be with. It was January, and we were looking forward to a fabulous family fling to celebrate Sam's, Erin's, and Mollie's upcoming birthdays.

My career had regained enough momentum to keep me com-fortably busy, even though many radio stations still wouldn't play my music, many churches had made it clear that I would never be invited to perform there again, and a lot of people in the music industry still kept their distance from me. I was really enjoying performing at the churches that did invite me, because I could tell by their response that those audiences really "got it" when it came to understanding what Jesus had taught about love and grace and forgiveness.

> *I really couldn't imagine how my life could get any better. Then I got that e-mail message.*

The really amazing thing was all the pops concerts and patriotic events I'd been invited to do. In fact, by 2004 I had sung for five presidents (including an event for President Carter after he left office) and performed in sev-eral network television specials on the Fourth of July, Christmas, Thanksgiving, and other holidays. Anderson University had awarded me an honorary doctorate, and most amazing of all, I had been named a 2004 inductee into the Gospel Music Association's Hall of Fame.

To be honest, I really couldn't imagine how my life could get any better.

Then I got that e-mail message.

In the years since his adoptive mother had died, leaving behind the papers that told him his birth mother's name, Don and I had often discussed what it would be like if he could find his birth family. Although he knew his birth mother's name—Virginia McGinnis—he had almost no other information. He had made a few tentative inquiries now and then, but nothing had come of it.

Then, in 1999, Don attended his high-school reunion back in West Virginia. He had graduated with a girl whose maiden name was McGinnis, and she was at the reunion. During the social time, he told her, "I think I might be related to you." He asked her if the facts of his story rang a bell with her. (Don hadn't known in high school that his birth mother's name was McGinnis; that's why he hadn't asked this question earlier.) Could there have been an aunt or a cousin or some other relative thirty-eight years ago who had a baby and gave it up for adoption? he asked.

The McGinnis classmate shook her head. "No, I don't know about anything like that," she said, "but I'll ask my dad." She promptly called her father, who was president of a bank in Huntington, and repeated Don's questions. He knew that Don wasn't related to *him,* but he also knew that the manager of one of the bank's branch offices was a woman whose maiden name was also McGinnis (although the two families weren't related). So he contacted her and asked, as Don had queried, "Does this story sound familiar to you? Do you know anyone in your family who might have had a baby and given it up for adoption?"

There was a pause, then the woman replied, "As a matter of fact, yes, it does sound familiar."

That bank manager, Bev White—we now call her Aunt Bev—

took the information the bank president offered and shared it with Virginia McGinnis's sister, Cathie McGinnis Adams.

But there the process stopped and lay dormant for nearly five years. Don's search for his birth mother had reopened a tender wound for his mother's sister, an ocean of grief, and she just wasn't able to let it go any further for a while. You see, Virginia McGinnis had indeed given birth to Don all those years ago. She had been in love with a handsome high-school football star, and when she found out she was pregnant, she probably hoped they might get married despite the less-than-perfect circumstances and become a young but love-filled family.

But it wasn't to be. The young couple's parents adamantly refused to let them marry; they were too young, and they had a lot more living to do before they settled down to raise a family. The football star was heading off to college and, without a doubt, a bright future. This was no time for marriage and a baby.

Attitudes about unwed mothers were much different then than they are today. To stay out of view of what might have been a harshly critical public, Virginia—her family called her Ginny—stayed with her grandmother throughout her pregnancy. She was not far from home, and her parents and her sister, Cathie, visited her and stood by her every step of the way. Ginny was seventeen when Don was born in St. Mary's Hospital in Huntington, West Virginia. Ginny's mother—now we know her as Don's grandmother—vividly remembers that night as being cold and windy.

Although Ginny wanted to keep the baby, she and her parents believed it would be best for all concerned if she agreed to give it up for adoption. Ginny's doctor was also the family physician for Don's adoptive parents; apparently he made the arrangements for the private adoption. Ginny's mother and father tried to see the baby boy (that's all they were told, that it was a boy), but when they went to the nursery, they were told that, since it was a private adoption, he was not available for "public" viewing; he wasn't in the nursery with the other babies. Ginny's mother believes to this day that if her husband had been able to see the baby, he would never have signed the papers that finalized Don's adoption.

A Lifetime of Searching

I can only image the grief Ginny and her family must have felt as they gave up that sweet little baby boy. It also makes me hold in the greatest admiration those birth mothers (like my little Sam's) who know they cannot provide the kind of home their child needs and deserves and so selflessly give him or her to the eagerly awaiting adoptive parents who have longed for a child to love and nurture.

Ginny had withdrawn from high school during her senior year to stay out of public view during her pregnancy. After Don was born, she returned to her hometown and got her diploma. By then the boyfriend had gone off to college; the two of them never got back together. In fact, there were some unpleasant encounters between them. Ginny eventually married someone else, and during that period of her life she tried to find the baby she had reluctantly given up. When this failed, so did her marriage. Adoption laws and state records at that time were sealed, and all doors to finding her son were firmly closed. She never had any more children. In 1969, when she was just twenty-six years old, she died in Los Angeles. Everyone who knew her believed she died of a broken heart.

It was all so sad, but for Don there also would be amazing joy in his mother's story, as I'll explain later.

Feeling the grief anew when she heard that Ginny's son was looking for his birth mother, Don's aunt (Ginny's sister), Cathie McGinnis Adams, at first could not bring herself to respond to the inquiry or to share the news with her mother, knowing it would reignite the painful heartache that had smoldered within the family all those years. Now that we know the full story, including parts of it that cannot be shared here, Don and I understand completely how difficult it must have been for them, and we grieve with them for the loss of their precious young Ginny.

Although Cathie wasn't ready to make contact when she first learned of Don's inquiry, she hung on to the information. And as the years went by, she eventually felt strong enough to do what needed to be done; she decided that Don deserved to know who his birth mom really was and how much she had loved and wanted him. So she made that first gesture to reach out to her sister's son. Because she doesn't own a computer, she asked her cousin Bev White for help. That's when the e-mail message appeared that would change Don's life forever.

Uncovering the Links

Shortly after that first tentative contact, an envelope addressed to Don arrived in our mail. Cathie and Bev had promised to send some family photographs, and Don sat on the couch holding that envelope for a long time before he opened it. It was such a tender yet powerful moment for him, realizing he was about to see his mother's face for the first time. He unfolded the letter, turned over the first photograph, and found his own intense eyes staring back at him. His first thought was, *She is so beautiful!* The second was, *She looks like my Aly.* Then, as a tear trickled down his face, he thought, *Oh, Mom. I wish you could meet your grandchildren.*

As soon as we could, we arranged to travel to Huntington to meet Aunt Cathie and her husband, Uncle Ralph, as well as Aunt Bev and her husband, Uncle Bruff. (They're technically Don's cousins, but everyone agreed that the honorary titles of *aunt* and *uncle* work better.) We brought along two of Don's kids, Donnie and Aly, and it was a beautiful time of love and discovery.

We drove to Huntington and spent the night in a downtown hotel across the street from the Marshall University Hall of Fame and Café, where we would meet Don's relatives the next day. We had reserved a small, private dining room, and as we walked in, Bev got to Don first, wrapping him in her arms. "You know what?" Don said, tears welling up in his eyes. "This is the first time in forty-three years I've been able to hug an adult who's related to me by blood."

His Aunt Cathie was eager for her hug too. "You look like your mother," she said, her voice full of tears and laughter as the two of them latched on to each other in a warm, long-overdue embrace.

How sweet it was to share that time with people who were all but strangers to us when we walked in but who instantly became family as we got to know one another. Don was touched to hear he shared the musical talents of his mother, who had played the guitar and sung with a beautiful voice. And it was sweet to hear the kids getting acquainted with their Aunt Cathie, Uncle Ralph, Aunt Bev, and Uncle Bruff. At first the youngsters were a bit shy, answering gentle questions with a smile and a few words. But before the day was over they were laughing and joking with their new family members as though they had grown up knowing them.

As he talked to his relatives and they got to know each other, Don was sometimes quiet and pensive, listening to his mother's story. He couldn't help but grieve, as they did, and hurt for his mother, learning the sad experiences she had endured. He was grieving for not one mother but two: the women he describes now as "the one who gave me life and the one who taught me how to live it." But there was also a bittersweet joy mixed in with the moments of mourning. For in God's amazing way of making all things work for good, Don had the answer to an unspoken question he had pondered for years.

> *"As an adopted child, you always wonder,* Did anybody love me?"

"As an adopted child, you always wonder, *Was I loved? Did anybody love me?*" he explained later. It's bittersweet to know that my mother loved me so much that she looked for me all those years—and died of a broken heart when she couldn't find me."

It was heartwarming for Don to meet his mother's relatives— Aunt Cathie and Uncle Ralph, as well as Aunt Bev and Uncle Bruff. Our time with them was full of laughter and, occasionally, tears. Next would come the meeting with his grandmother, Ginny's mother. She was at her winter home in Florida when we first made contact with Cathie and Bev and their husbands. Cathie was very protective of her mother, not wanting to cause her any more grief, and had decided not to mention Don to her until she (Cathie) could meet him herself. She wanted to have enough information to make the meeting between grandmother and grandson go as smoothly as possible.

She managed it all beautifully. When that moment came a few months later, Don's sweet grandmother opened her arms to him and held him close as tears flowed down her smooth cheeks. And hers weren't the only cheeks in that room that glistened with tears. Soon laughter abounded as well. Don's grandmother was obviously tickled to death to be united with her grandson. She delighted in telling him about his mother as well as about his great-grandmother (Grandmother's mother), a petite, dark-haired beauty with "a lot of Indian in her," Grandmother said, "and the most beautiful jet black eyes." Everyone was also struck by Don's amazing resemblance to his Grandfather McGinnis, who had died several years earlier.

What a wonderful time we had, getting to know Don's "new" relatives. Only a few weeks earlier he had been an "orphaned" only child whose loving parents had died. Now he had gained the family he had dreamed of for so long but never knew how to find. In fact, even today he has cousins and relatives on his mother's side whom we still haven't met, simply because it's been difficult to find a time when everyone could be in the same place at the same time. So we have those additional discoveries to look forward to.

As Don got acquainted with his mother's family, it was inevitable that he would want to know, "Who was my dad?"

His grandmother and aunts could give him only a few sketchy details. They had had no contact with the young man who had fathered their loved one's baby since those final, difficult days so long ago. But they remembered his name: Jim Perry.

As we shared Don's mind-boggling experience with our friends and family members, something interesting happened. Don has remained good friends with his first wife, Michelle, and her family. In fact, another one of Don's friends is Michelle's brother-in-law Wally Booth, who is married to Michelle's sister Denise.

Wally and Denise live in Detroit, but he is from West Virginia, and he just happened to know some Perrys who live in Huntington. Don asked Wally and Denise if they would be willing to help us make contact with those Huntington Perrys. Denise said that Wally's niece, who lived in Huntington, just happened to be best friends with Barbie LaValley, whose maiden name is Smith and—stay with me, now—whose mother's maiden name is Perry. When Wally's niece called Barbie and shared the story, Barbie replied, "Well, I have an uncle Jim Perry. Let me see what I can find out."

Positive Proof

Don wasn't home when Barbie called our house, but we had talked about what he wanted to do if and when one of Wally's contacts called us. So I followed the steps he had laid out. Listening to Barbie explain who she was, I had the feeling that something extraordinary was about to happen. Still, Jim Perry isn't all that unusual a name. There were probably lots of Jim Perrys out there, and we knew this might not be the right one. I tried to hold my excitement in check as I briefly gave her some identifying facts about Don's life and asked her to call her uncle.

Barbie called her uncle Jim and told him she had heard from a family who was wondering . . . It was an awkward question to ask . . . Well, they were wondering if he might be the father of a boy who had been adopted at birth.

"Before you say anything else," Jim answered, "let me ask you: was he born March 8, 1961?"

Barbie gasped.

"I've been looking for him all my life," he said, his voice nearly breaking.

The next stage was the most delicate, something best left to the women to arrange. Jim and Don knew it seemed likely that they were father and son, but they wanted to keep their hearts guarded until they were certain. So they agreed to go for DNA testing. Barbie and I made the arrangements. We learned that things would go faster if the DNA sample could be taken and tested in the same facility. Don and I traveled to West Virginia so a lab there could do both tests. The two appointments were on different days.

After the technician swabbed Don's cheek for the cell sample, Don said earnestly, "Sir, I want to ask you something. It's important to me. When you get the results, will you call me first? I want to know, because I want to be able to call my dad and say, 'Hello, Dad, this is your son.'"

We went home to Indiana, and Jim went in to have his sample taken the next day. When the technician was finished, Jim said to him, "Sir, this is really important. When you get the results, I want you to call me first, because I want to be able to call my son and say, 'Hello, Don. This is your dad.'"

(At that point, the technician told us later, he wanted to say, "I could save you both a lot of money, because from what I've seen, you two *are* related!")

It took a week for the tests to be completed. The technicians would look at fifteen DNA sites. If seven of the fifteen matched, that would be considered a very, very strong positive. When they looked at Don and Jim's samples, fifteen of the fifteen sites matched.

The lab called Jim first.

Don and I were in Baltimore for a concert when we got the news. Baltimore Symphony Orchestra conductor Jack Everly had set up the event, and he had invited Don to sing "The Prayer" with me. We got the message about the test results that afternoon, and right before we were to leave for the concert, Don and his dad heard each other's voices for the first time.

Sitting in the room as father and son had their first conversation, I was so delighted to hear Don call someone *Dad* for the first time in more than thirty years, since his adoptive dad had died in 1972.

"That's right, Dad," he said. "I know, Dad." And later I heard him say, "You're so right, Dad."

What an amazing thing had happened to us. That night, singing the beautiful lyrics of "The Prayer" with Don was an especially significant and special moment for both of us as we rejoiced that a father had been found, a son had been claimed, and a new relationship had begun.

Pop

Don and his father had first talked on Friday. They also talked on Saturday. And Sunday. And Monday. Sometimes they talked several times a day. They just kept thinking of things they wanted to ask and tell each other. Obviously a face-to-face meeting had to be arranged as soon as possible. We all looked at our calendars and chose Valentine's Day weekend.

Our whole family was excited to meet this new, central character in Don's life. We cleaned the house until it was spotless; the kids even cleaned their rooms until they were spotless. OK, so I may have gone a little psycho, acting like a drill sergeant with the kids, but hey, this was a big moment in our family history. Anyway, the house looked good. I even hung up all the piles of clothes that usually reside on the floor of my closet.

Jim was going to drive from West Virginia, and Don decided he would meet him halfway. Anna and her boyfriend, Collin, offered to take Don to the rendezvous point, then Don would hop in the car with Jim and they would drive to Anderson together. That way they would have a chance to really talk one-on-one before Jim entered the craziness of our big, loud family.

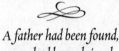

A father had been found, a son had been claimed, and a new relationship had begun.

Both cars arrived right on time. Don got out of Anna's car; then the door of the other car opened, and there was Jim. Anna said it was like watching a slow-motion scene in a movie as the two men moved toward each other. Then they were all hugging and crying and laughing at the same time. What a moment.

On the way to Anderson, Don and his dad talked nonstop for two hours, relishing their discovery of all the things they had in common. Don called us when they were about ten minutes away so we could put the finishing touches on the house. We took turns peeking through the curtains, watching for their arrival. When they finally pulled into the driveway, the kids and I were suddenly nervous, for some reason. But as soon as we saw Don's dad and his broad, warm smile, we all relaxed.

He told us to call him Pop, and we just loved that. What a perfect term of endearment for this special family member who popped into our lives like a special gift from heaven.

Pop is a hugger, and we all got our hugs one at a time. When it was Sam's turn, Pop gave him a big hug, then Sam said, "Hey, Pop, look what I can do." And he proceeded to put his hand under his armpit and make that special bodily function sound eight-year-old boys love to make. We all laughed at Sam's trick, which turned out to be a great icebreaker, in a wacky sort of way.

We hurriedly showed Pop around the house. (I explained that we only had a short window of time before it looked "lived in" again.) When we got to Erin's room, Don and Pop paused and looked out Erin's westward-facing window. The late afternoon view over the wintry field was ablaze with glorious color. Almost simultaneously both of them commented that this was their favorite part of the day. As they stood there, watching the sun go down, Pop put his arm around Don and said, "Son, this is our first sunset together."

Pop brought gifts to give us. He had an especially poignant gift for Don's girls, Aly and Mollie (his first granddaughters—and he considers my three girls, Anna, Jenni, and Erin, his granddaughters too, so in the blink of an eye, he went from zero to five granddaughters). Because his sister, Mabel, and Ginny, Don's birth mother, had been close friends, they had shared a lot of high-school treasures. They both had worn identical Indian spirit necklaces, and as a gift to Mollie and Aly, Pop brought Ginny's necklace that Mabel had saved all those years.

Telling the Story

A few weeks later, Don went alone to West Virginia to return Pop's visit. I called him about bedtime and asked, "What are you doing?"

He chuckled. "Well, Dad's tucking me in. He's sitting here with me. He . . ." There was a catch in Don's voice. "He brought me some milk and cookies. He wanted to tuck me in and tell me a bedtime story—to make up for all the times he couldn't do it when I was growing up."

The story Jim told that night was Don's story—the story of his birth parents. He said, "If you ever wondered, . . . you were conceived in tremendous love."

Pop's sister, Mabel, had helped Ginny and Pop sneak around so they could be together more than their parents wanted them to. Pop and Ginny loved being together, and they especially enjoyed dancing. Pop was eighteen when Ginny told him she was pregnant. Doing what they thought was best for both children, their parents relocated both teenagers, hoping their romance would cool as Ginny lived with her grandmother while awaiting the baby's arrival. He didn't forget about her, Pop told Don, "But I didn't stand by her as I should have."

Pop had been a young, gifted athlete, and his parents were putting a lot of pressure on him to go on to college and make a life for himself when Ginny became pregnant. "Not that I'm saying that to make excuses," he added. "It's just what happened."

Throughout his life, Don had heard rumors that his birth father had played football for Marshall University. Perhaps feeling a subconscious pull to connect with his father, Don had always been a huge fan of Marshall's football team. In fact, I teased him for years that his was the only car in Indiana to have a Marshall Thundering Herd license plate. Now his attraction to the school's football team took on even more meaning. It was touching to think that when we met with Don's Aunt Cathie and Aunt Bev and their husbands that first day in the university's Hall of Fame Café, without knowing it, we were standing near the photo of Pop's football team.

Pop had come into Don's life at what felt like exactly the right time.

Pop had enjoyed his days at Marshall. While he was there, he fell in love and married a beautiful young woman who reigned as Marshall's homecoming queen one year. They got married, reared a family, and Pop, with his engineering degree, worked for the DuPont Corporation setting up electronic plants all over the world. His sons spent many of their growing-up years in Singapore. Now divorced and retired, Pop had come into Don's life at what felt like exactly the right time, when he had time to enjoy his newly expanded family. And Don, whose adoptive parents had both died, was now in his early forties and the father of (among other children) an adopted son, so he had new insights and a different appreciation for his biological father than he might have had if the two had discovered each other earlier in life. Considering how perfect the timing was, you might think God had a hand in it!

Putting the Puzzle Together

As Don learned more about his family of origin, a lot of facts fell into place for him; reasons became clear for why he had become the man he is today. For example, fitness has always been important to him; he had made it his career when he was working for the YMCA. As a boy he had always enjoyed sports, but his overly protective mother had forbidden him to play the sport he'd really wanted to play: football. I think she felt that since her husband had passed away, she just didn't want to take any chances with her only child. For Don, finding out that his birth father had been a high-school and college football star verified to him that he had inherited a natural inclination toward athletics.

Then there are the physical characteristics that now are explained. When Pop came to visit us, he came into the kitchen barefoot the first morning. I had to laugh when I saw him. "You've got Don's feet!" I told him.

Here's another thing: now that Don knows he has Native American genes from his mother's side, he understands why he tans so easily and so deeply every summer.

Most amazing of all, he sees in his children the characteristics of his own birth parents. Looking at the old family pictures, Don sees that his daughter Aly, for instance, is a gorgeous look-alike for her beautiful grandmother, Ginny. Mollie looks like her grandmother's sisters. Donnie looks just like Don's brother Jim when he was younger. (Technically Pop's four other sons are Don's *half*-brothers, of course, but you'll never hear Don call them that!)

It was an incredible experience to look into those faces, either in photographs or in person, and see such strong resemblances in the young faces of his children. But there's another extraordinary part of this story, and that is the framework it gave Sam for understanding his own adoption. He could already see that he had an adoptive family that was head-over-heels crazy about him, but he got an added understanding that he was genetically related to a whole other family out there whom he might want to search for someday.

Well, OK, Sam's understanding might still lack a little scientific information. That became evident recently when Don was having trouble with his knees. One morning during that time Sam woke up and complained that his knee kind of hurt too. I rubbed his leg and expressed some concern, and he explained to me, "You know, Mom, I think it's an adopted thing."

Yes, it was all an amazing experience: Don lost his father when he was eleven years old and regained a father when he was forty-three. But perhaps the biggest change of all was that, while Don had been raised as an only child with very few extended family members, all of a sudden he had four brothers and three active nephews who would be calling him Uncle Don.

Learning about his brothers has also given Don insights into his own character and makeup. All four of them are active and successful. Jim is a Miami attorney and loves to go boating on the weekends; John has a degree in design and, in my opinion, could be one of those awesome decorators on *Trading Spaces*; and Richie is a computer genius working on the miniaturization of microprocessors in Portland, Oregon. And then there's Lenny, who very well may have passed Don on the sidewalk a time or two in the last couple of years.

You see, Don attended summer school the last few summers, working toward his master's degree in character education. One of the only schools in America that offers that degree is the University of San Diego, a small Catholic college on a beautiful campus in California where—guess what—Lenny, a PhD, just happens to be a member of the faculty. In summer 2004 Don lived with Lenny for six weeks as he worked to finish his degree.

And in the middle of last summer, we met the rest of the clan at the annual family reunion in Miami. What an experience it was for Don, an only child, to suddenly be in the midst of a new mob of fun-loving family members who were related to him through blood or marriage. Don, Sam, and I went to Miami for the occasion, and I have to admit I was a little nervous about making the trip.

OK, let's be honest: I was freaking out. I knew I would be *way* out of my comfort zone; I pictured myself being surrounded by strangers while being expected to act like they were family. All of those fears evaporated as soon as we emerged from the airport concourse and were met by my sister-in-law, Sue, who wrapped her arms around us and gave us the grandest welcome imaginable. Her three boys ran up to Sam and started chattering away about all the stuff he and his new cousins would be doing over the next few days.

It was the most wonderful weekend. Don's new family embraced us as though we'd been coming to those reunions for decades. Sam had a blast running around with the horde of cousins. And then there was that afternoon on the beach when a couple of the guys started throwing a football around.

As I said earlier, Don had wanted to play football as a teenager, and although his mother hadn't allowed it, he had kept wondering, in the back of his mind, whether he would be good at it. Now here he was, the son of a collegiate football star, with his four newly found brothers, all of whom had played football throughout their growing-up years. And the football was being tossed around . . .

The game of catch soon turned into a game of what the guys called two-hand-touch football (but looked more like two-hand-shove football to me). As far as I could tell, the teams were the oldest versus the youngest, and Don was the oldest brother of all. I must say that he and the other "old" guys looked mighty fine out there diving for catches, blocking the other team, intercepting, tackling—er, two-hand touching. Don even scored a couple of touchdowns. It was a sight to behold. My smile got wider and wider as I watched the moment unfold. Then I just couldn't help it. I yelled out to him, in front of everybody, "Hey, Don! You're playing football *with your brothers!*"

I thought I saw a few tears twinkling in his eyes, but I'm not sure if it was because he was feeling emotional—or because he was getting pummeled.

All that I've done before won't matter anymore.
—Bill and Gloria Gaither, Danny Daniels
"I've Just Seen Jesus"

Chapter Thirteen

ON THE ROAD AGAIN

The church's sanctuary was set up differently than any other I had ever seen. Picture a large, rectangular room that seats about thirty-five hundred people, and then imagine a stage smack-dab in the middle. Looking at the setup before showtime, I couldn't help but feel a tiny bit of apprehension.

Chonda Pierce had invited me to join her in a hilarious, Spirit-filled concert tour we called The Girls Are Back in Town, and we had laughed and sung our way all over Middle America, celebrating and sharing the marvelous ways God had worked in our lives. Because of the unusual setup in this particular church—not exactly "in the round" but rather "front or back"—we had the audience watching both sides of us. It was a little worrisome, because Chonda and I love to connect with the audience, and in that setting it felt like if we connected with one side, we were leaving out the other.

Fortunately (or maybe unfortunately) the church had four large video screens, two on each side. The thing is, with video, if you turn too fast, the camera can't keep up. The show got off to its usual raucous, rollicking start, and each time I turned too fast, for about ten very long seconds, my backside was as big as day for all thirty-five hundred people to see on those video screens. (And did I mention that we chose each other's outfits for each half of the show? For the opening half, I had selected lovely tailored outfits that made us look like the divas we are. For the second half,

At home my closet is organized by sizes: 14, 16, 18, and "none of your business."

Chonda had dressed me like one hot mama in the coolest leather pants you've ever seen. I loved them—as viewed from the front.)

It's no secret that I struggle with my body image. It seems like I am always on a diet. It just doesn't come easily for me. At home my closet is organized by sizes: 14, 16, 18, and "none of your business." My daughters, Anna, Jenni, and Erin, and my stepdaughters, Aly and Mollie, have grown into beautiful young ladies who are tall and thin, with gorgeous, long legs. I tell them, "My darlings, as your mother I am so proud of you. However, as a woman I hate your guts."

Just kidding. I know I gave birth to at least three of these beauties, but I just want you to know that I saved all the good stuff for them.

Anyway, there I was, standing up on that stage with at least half of the audience seeing the worst part of my body all the time. And, you now, the camera adds at least ten pounds. It's just not fair. But there wasn't anything I could do about it. I couldn't wear a longer coat and pretend the worst side of me wasn't there. I couldn't wear a girdle tight enough to hide the flaws, and I've sworn off control-top pantyhose. A few years ago I was performing in the round, so there was no place to hide when those darn pantyhose started going south. I stopped the concert, excused myself to the audience, slipped down the steps onto the floor of the arena, pulled the backup singers into an outward-facing circle around me, and hitched 'em up. Thank goodness it was an audience of mostly women.

That night with Chonda in that front-and-back venue, I just had to be what I was and reveal the truth about myself. My backside is always there, even if I don't actually have to see it all the time, but that night I saw it over and over again whenever I caught a glimpse of myself on the screen. And to make it worse, all night I had to stand beside cute little size-six Chonda, who always looks adorable on stage.

Surrounded by those huge video screens, I felt like all my flaws were bigger than life. The truth is, they were. I could pretend they weren't there, but the camera doesn't lie. The cool thing about all of this was I never felt the audience was thinking, *Oh, bless her heart. Look at that poor girl's backside. Look at all her flaws being revealed to everyone. I'd better turn my head and look away.*

No, there was none of that. They looked me in the eye, and they affirmed and loved me, flaws and all. They offered me total and unconditional acceptance.

Remind you of Anyone you know?

The experience was an immediate analogy of my life. God has

loved me and accepted me, just as I am, flaws and all. He doesn't turn His head and look away. He looks me in the eye and calls me His child. It reminds me of the song by Phil McHugh that I used to sing a few years ago:

> In Heaven's eyes, there are no losers.
> In Heaven's eyes, no hopeless cause,
> Only people like you
> With feelings like me.
> And we're amazed by the grace we can find
> In Heaven's eyes.

There is no story more powerful than that. And there was no one more gracious about publicly living it out with me than Chonda. When she asked if I would be interested in doing the tour with her, I said to her, "Do you know about my past? Do you know that I made some bad choices? Do you know that some people may stop listening to you because you are with me?"

"Are you talking about the stuff from twelve years ago?" Chonda asked.

"That's what I'm talking about," I told her.

"Good Lord! Twelve years ago I was workin' in a bar!" she answered.

So there we were, two gals hitting the road for Jesus, ready to show the world what redemption looks like. Chonda was such a powerful influence and encourager. Not only did she fill my days with laughter, she gave me a whole new perspective on what the life of a Christian entertainer is all about. When a woman commented that when Chonda was on stage, she seemed to be working for the Lord, Chonda corrected her. "No, I *live my life* for the Lord," she said. "I *work* for those people out there in the audience."

When the tour was about to end, we were having so much fun and the audiences were so receptive, we just added more dates and kept on going.

The Journey Continues

And so the journey from the back row of the balcony continues—and now includes the huge, welcoming audiences at Women of Faith conferences around the country. The first one I was invited to was in Fort Lauderdale in 2004. Chonda was there, watching from the front row, along with two other extraordinary friends, Women of Faith speaker–team member Sheila Walsh and guest artist Kathy Troccoli.

When I walked on stage and looked around at the cavernous arena and the eleven thousand women gathered there, I felt an immediate peace. I sensed that all of us in that place had been wounded in some way and that we were all pulling together and affirming that yes, we serve the God of second chances—and third and fourth chances and on into infinity. I began my segment of the program, and as if to encourage me and embrace me with validation and love, the women in the hearing-impaired section stood and signed with me as I sang the song "We Shall Behold Him." My eyes filled with tears as we "sang" together, and as I left the stage, I reminded them, "and every ear shall hear!"

Sheila met me at the bottom of the steps as I came off the stage, then Chonda and Kathy rushed me, and we hugged and laughed and cried and jumped up and down as the audience cheered, and we all kept saying, "Isn't God good? Isn't He cool?"

I felt so welcomed and so loved. It kind of reminded me of the prodigal son when he came home. He knew he wanted to be back with his family, but he felt so ashamed for all he had put them through. He was ready to face the consequences so he could get his life back on the right track. But when he came home, it wasn't wrath he received, but a welcome. It wasn't lashing out, it was love poured onto him. His father didn't knock him senseless; instead he killed the fatted calf and celebrated his son's return.

> *There were many years when I was singing, but I wasn't happy and I wasn't free. . . . Maybe you've been there too.*

That's the kind of welcome those women in the arena gave me that day. I can only hope they realize just how God used them to touch my heart. It is a moment that has been imprinted on my memory forever.

In that place I felt the same feelings, on a much larger scale, I have felt ever since my fall into sin and my slow, torturous recovery from the stain it left on my life. I am honored when I'm invited to come and sing, whether it's at a little-bitty church or a large arena. I get choked up when I talk about it. I don't take it for granted like I used to. I'm humbled and grateful that they want me to come, with all my battle scars, to share what God has done for me.

And His faithfulness continues. One morning recently I opened Max Lucado's wonderful devotional *Everyday Blessings* and found, as the reading for the day, Jesus's words in Mark 16:7: "Go, tell his disciples and Peter, 'He is going ahead of you into Galilee.'"

Under that passage Max had written, "If I might paraphrase the words, 'Don't stay here. Go tell the disciples,' a pause, then a smile, 'and especially Peter, that he is going before you to Galilee.' . . . It's as if all of heaven had watched Peter fail—and it's as if all of heaven wanted to help him back up again. . . . No wonder they call it the Gospel of the second chance."

Whether they know it or not, those women—and all of the people who come to hear me—are helping me back up again. They know God's grace redeemed me and gave me a second chance, and I guess everyone loves a story with a happy ending, especially when they know that ending is just as available for them as it is for me.

A Legacy of Love and Truth

I love the song "His Eye Is on the Sparrow," especially the lines that say,

> I sing because I'm happy.
> I sing because I'm free.
> For His eye is on the sparrow, and
> I know He watches me.

These days I sing that song a lot, and those lyrics bring me to tears nearly every time. You see, there were many years when I was singing, but I wasn't happy and I wasn't free. I sang because I had to. That was the season of my life when I sat on the back row of the balcony, feeling far from God, and all I could do was cry.

Maybe you've been there too. Maybe you're there right now. I want you to know, God can find you there. Reach out to Him, seek His forgiveness, cling to His mercy, and you too can enjoy the awesome, unbelievable freedom that only the truth can bring.

Be merciful, just as your Father is merciful.
Do not judge, and you will not be judged.
Do not condemn, and you will not be condemned.
Forgive, and you will be forgiven.
Give, and it will be given to you.
A good measure, pressed down, shaken together
and running over, will be poured into your lap.
For with the measure you use, it will be measured to you.

—*Luke 6:36–38*

Epilogue

A SECOND CHANCE

Anderson, Indiana

September 2004

It's nearly midnight, and the house is finally quiet. Don is in Miami with his brothers and his father, who's scheduled to undergo an angioplasty between hurricanes. The kids are all asleep, and the dogs are curled up on their big floor cushion. It's my favorite time of the day, when I finally have a few moments to myself. Usually this is a time of peace and contentment. But tonight my face is streaked with tears.

The manuscript for this book came back today from my editor, and as I read the whole thing through once more, all the shame and hurt came sweeping over me again. It was as though a cold north wind chilled my being as the sin in my life smacked me in the face yet again. Reading the difficult story of my wrong and sinful choices, I wondered, *How could anyone do this to her family?* And then to think *I'm* the one who did it! The realization is devastating each time my mind probes that terrible memory. Despite the late hour, I called my parents and apologized once more for the embarrassment and pain I had caused them. In the morning I'll tell my kids again how sorry I am for what I've put them through.

And then, watching them happily head off to school, I'll smile and thank God again for His precious gift of grace.

If you've also tasted that wonderful gift, if you've made that long, difficult journey back from the top row of the balcony, you know what I'm talking about. You've probably shed some of those midnight tears just as I have. But the gift of grace assures you that God's joy will be waiting for you in the morning.

Never forget that He can find you, no matter how deeply you're mired in the muck.

Everyone has a story. Maybe yours isn't as destructive or as traumatic as mine. I hope not. But if it is, I hope this book has encouraged you to reach out to God no matter how far you've fallen. Never forget that He can find you, no matter how deeply you're mired in the muck.

And if you know someone who's stuck there on the back row of life's balcony, broken by sin and filled with despair, I hope my story will help you minister to that person. It's so important, when you've made a huge mistake and fallen into sin, to know that you're not alone and that there's someone who's willing to walk beside you as you make that journey back to wholeness.

My family and my church were tremendously helpful to me as I worked toward restoration. Hoping now to be equally helpful to *you*, I've asked Pastor Lyon to add his own little postscript of encouragement at the end of this book. While many churches are fully prepared to facilitate their wayward parishioners' restoration to the body of Christ, others might not be so carefully equipped. Pastor Lyon's suggestions are there for you if you and your church need help in setting up this kind of procedure.

A Final Word

Going back through my story again has stirred up a lot of emotions within me. It also brought to mind an insightful question an interviewer asked me not too long ago. She asked me how I want to be remembered. I considered her question awhile, thinking about all I had been through and how the truth had set me free from all the dark times and brought me to the happy, holy season of life I enjoy today. Of course I couldn't say all that. Epitaphs have to be short. So I answered this way:

> Sandi Patty was a woman who sought after God with her whole heart, who loved her family and her friends. And when she got the chance, she sang about it.

Now I run through fields of mercy,
I fly through skies of grace,
I drink the Living Water that won't run dry,
I hide under the shadow of the Almighty God,
And I dwell in the presence of the Most High Almighty God.
—J. D. Webb
"Fields of Mercy"

PS

FINDING YOUR WAY
BACK TO HOPE

If you're feeling broken right now and you end up crying on the back row at church some Sunday, I hope you will feel God's reassuring presence of love. He has promised to forgive you for whatever sin you have committed. All you have to do is confess that sin to Him, repent of it, ask His forgiveness, and it will be given.

After that, you and your church may feel, as I did in my church, that certain steps would be beneficial in helping you work your way back to wholeness and restoration to the body of Christ. If so, I hope your church is prepared and equipped, as mine was, to help you take those steps. I've asked my pastor to share with you some of the insights and procedures a church might consider when a member of the congregation seeks such restoration. This message is adapted with permission from Pastor Jim Lyon's chapter in *First Steps to Ministry: A Primer on a Life in Christian Ministry.* And so he writes . . .

Moral failure among God's people is nothing new; biblical history is littered with it. Samson failed. Saul failed. David failed. Solomon failed. Jonah failed. The Hebrews failed. All twelve of the disciples of Jesus failed; Peter failed spectacularly. All committed willful, disobedient sin, abiding and abetting the enemy after having once pledged fidelity to God. In both Testaments, the evidence of failure is both overwhelming and sobering.

Restoration is more than massaging broken hearts and bringing closure to sad chapters in life; it is refusing to surrender any of heaven's own to hell's work.

But equally overwhelming is the evidence that God is in the restoration business. The gospel is the astonishing record of the Lord's effort to reclaim, to redeem, and to restore those who were originally His but who, in time, were lost. Luke 15 outlines with compelling clarity the passion and focus on restoration in God's kingdom. The lost sheep, the lost coin, the lost son—and the intense efforts to redeem them—are at the core of this series of revealing parables.

The potential for restoration plainly exists. First Timothy 2:3–4 NASB talks of "God, our Savior, who desires all men to be saved and to come to the knowledge of the truth." Elsewhere the Scripture commands "those who are spiritual" to "restore" any "caught in any trespass" (Galatians 1:6 NASB). There are com-

mon scriptural threads that herald restoration; these threads out-
line processes and responsibilities that, if embraced, release the
backslidden from their bondage and restore them to the Lord's
employ. Restoration is more than massaging broken hearts and
bringing closure to sad chapters in life; it is refusing to surrender
any of heaven's own to hell's work—redeploying wounded soldiers
(remade whole) into constructive ministry for the glory of God.

Restoration is not only possible, it is encouraged and hoped
for. But in the biblical stories, not all who stray are restored to the
body of Christ. What separates the restored from the doomed?
Five things.

1. Honest and Straightforward Acknowledgment of Failure

Restoration hinges on the honest and straightforward admission
of the wayward soul's failure. Sin can never be addressed if it is
not named. It cannot be purged if it is not identified. It cannot be
cleaned if it cannot be seen.

Occasionally we comprehend our sin alone. By the prompting
of the Spirit and the channel of conscience, we understand our
failure without the help of an outside voice. Guilt, shame, and loss
of peace all creep into our souls and remind us of our error. Others
may not be aware that we are lifting cash from the choir's offering,
but we know. We fear discovery. We comprehend our sin.

More often than not, however, we rationalize our sin, deluding
ourselves into believing that our behavior is acceptable or, at least,
not reprehensible. We refuse to look at ourselves honestly, we

ignore the silent stirring of our muted conscience, and we avoid responsibility. We become defensive when questioned and find ourselves working harder to maintain the facade of propriety. The performance becomes exhausting, but we continue acting, day after day, postponing the inevitable.

In either case, confession must take place, either at the prompting of the Spirit in the sinner's heart or by the approach of another member of the body of Christ, following the commands of Matthew 18:15 and Galatians 6:1.

Confession is the cleansing of the wound, the forcing to the surface of the infection that has festered and stained the soul. It can be excruciating, but there is no other way for restoration to begin. Confession must be clear and straightforward. It cannot be couched in excuses or minimized by self-serving context. This confession must be made to God, of course, but it should also be made to the body of Christ (perhaps by disclosing to a member in authority who represents the whole congregation). As a general rule, confession also should be made to anyone directly injured by our sin.

Displaying our dirty laundry before the whole church is not usually necessary in confession. But confessing to a church representative can be a powerful step toward restoration. Pastors, naturally, find themselves in the role of confessor for parishioners from time to time. But carefully prepared church councils (where pledges of confidentiality are embraced) or specifically constituted confessional small groups can also play important roles when the wounded soldier needs more than a pastor can provide. Revealing personal failure in an appropriate setting allows him or her to believe that the body of Christ will recognize his or her restoration.

Confession to God opens the door for the Lord's forgiveness. Confession to the church opens the door for the church's forgiveness.

2. *Repentance*

To repent is to change course, to reverse direction. Once confession has been made (and forgiveness received), repentance must be demonstrated. An unequivocal commitment to turn away from the offending behavior must be made.

As with confession, the commitment to repent is most effective when made before other members representing the church. Our promises in these confidential groups bind and empower us in ways private promises do not. In the same way a marriage vow is made before witnesses, a renewed commitment to walk with Christ is best made before witnesses.

A specific plan outlining how the penitent will walk uprightly will maximize success. Accountability systems have great power to guard our steps. The group can help identify weaknesses, circumstances, and vulnerabilities and help steer a clear course. Engaging another member of the church to work with us in being faithful is wise. Such "repentance plans" may be necessary for months or years, depending on the nature of the infraction and personal history, but every effort at restoration needs such a plan.

3. *Restitution*

Some sins require restitution, the attempt to restore the loss someone else has suffered by our hand. Restitution typically involves a formal apology to the injured party and evidence of the offender's intent to repent. It may involve a financial compensation or a promise to perform some service or good work.

Restitution helps the wounded soldier understand that restoration is possible. The body of Christ should play an instrumental role in identifying and implementing any restitution arrangements. The church, through its appointed representatives, can fairly judge the propriety and satisfaction of the restitution effort. Once authenticated by the church, the person being restored can more readily accept closure with the injured party when restitution takes place.

4. Loving Discipline

The procedures outlined here are reinforced by the church body's loving discipline, including such requirements as: (a) regular reporting on the restitution progress, (b) routine meetings with mentors or counselors, and/or (c) assigned reading materials.

Most local churches are ill equipped to deliver loving discipline; we are loath to make formal judgments about others or become involved in ongoing, potentially awkward disciplinary relationships. Still, by stepping up to the challenge, churches can help redeem wounded soldiers and strengthen their ministry. Establishing accountability partners, accountability small groups (of three or four persons, appointed by some church authority), and/or disciplinary policies for restoration can be of great benefit. Loving discipline requires a commitment on the part of the church's leadership to stand fast and consistently in implementing its policies.

In the face of the offending sin, those representing the church must show sincere humility, with each one acknowledging, "There, but for the grace of God, go I." Discipline must never be punitive but redemptive. It must never be judgmental but forgiving. It must never be born from pride but delivered with modesty.

5. Restoration Closure

When honest and straightforward confession has been made, repentance has been owned and demonstrated, restitution has been pursued and completed, and a structure of loving discipline has been enforced, a formal end to the process should be recognized by the church. The memory of the sin should be sealed and removed from all conversation, and a celebration of the Lord's goodness and mercy should be enjoyed. The wounded soldier, now remade whole, should take his or her place back on the front line, free of the past and empowered spiritually to face the future.

No two circumstances are alike. Universal principles are the province of Scripture alone. General rules, though, do have validity. Most wounded soldiers can be restored to their original rank in heaven's army if the appropriate steps are taken over a sufficient period of time.

Above the fractures in our lives, the sovereign plan of God unfolds, through and beyond the restoration process. In Christ, we live abundantly. Without Him, we step backward into the darkness. And when we come to our senses (as did the prodigal in Luke 15), we, by the grace of God and the restorative process with God's people, can step back into the purposes for which He originally created us. We can fight, once more, on the Lord's side.

—Pastor Jim Lyon

CREDITS

NOTES

CHAPTER FOUR: RIDING FAME'S ROLLER COASTER

1. Lana Bateman is the founder of Philippian Ministries, an outreach of emotional-healing prayer designed to bring encouragement, growth, and healing for God's hurting children. For information contact Philippian Ministries, Inc., 9234 Firelog Lane, Dallas, TX 75243.

CHAPTER EIGHT: UGLY TRUTH, BEAUTIFUL FREEDOM

1. To order an audiotape of the complete sermon, write to North Anderson Church of God, PO Box 2479, Anderson, IN 46018-2479 and ask for Pastor Lyon's sermon preached on September 3, 1995. Please include $10 for postage and handling.